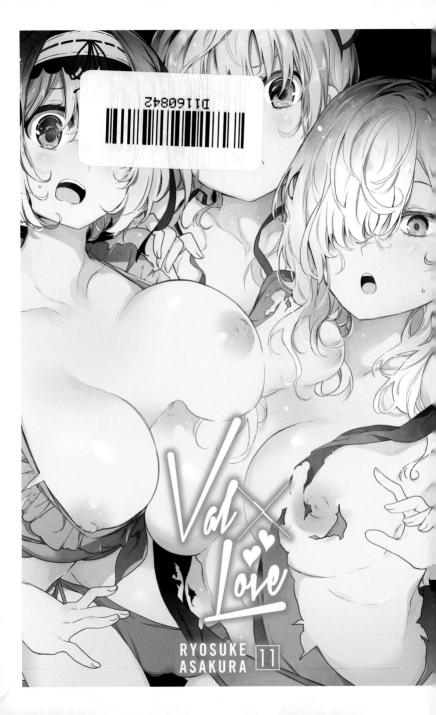

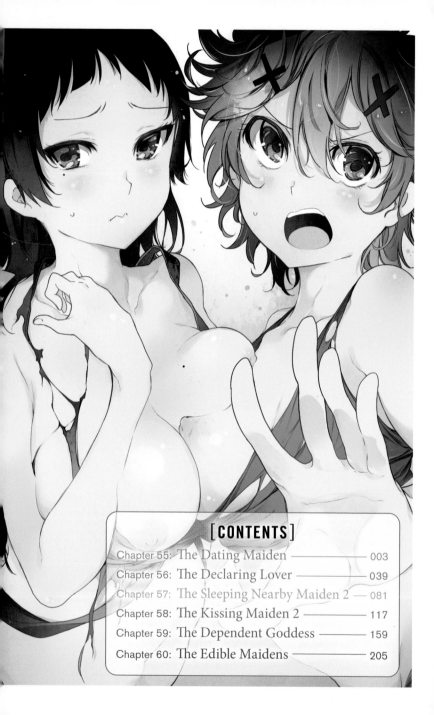

[CONTENTS]

Chapter 55: The Dating Maiden

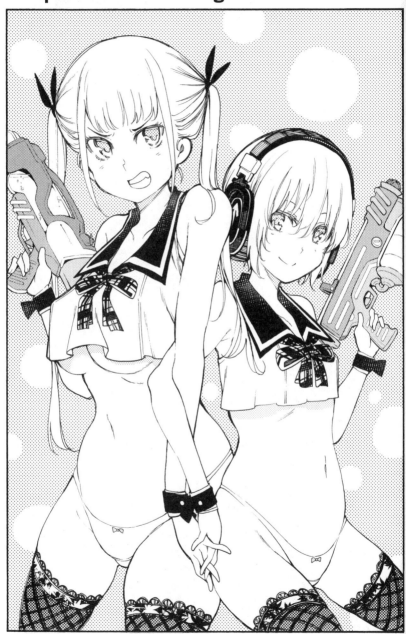

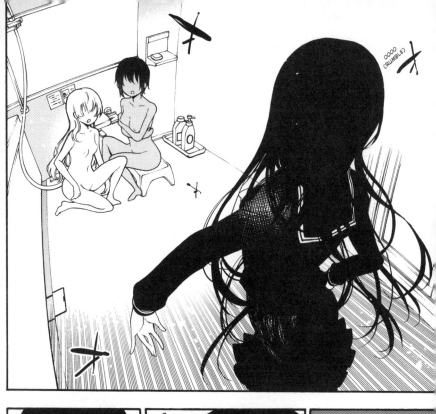

OOOO
(RUMBLE)

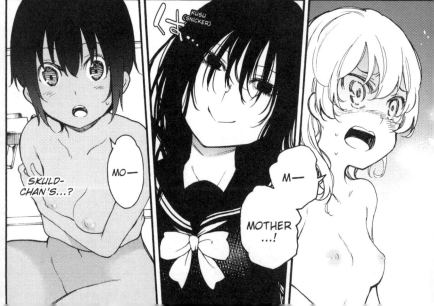

SKULD-
CHAN'S...?

MO—

KUSU
(SNICKER)

M—

MOTHER
...!

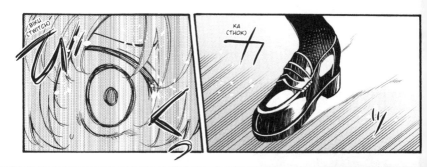

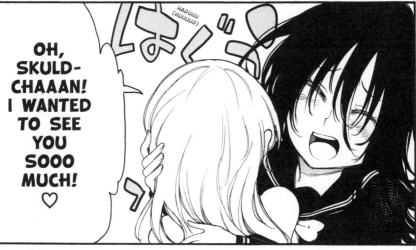

OH, SKULD-CHAAAN! I WANTED TO SEE YOU SOOO MUCH! ♡

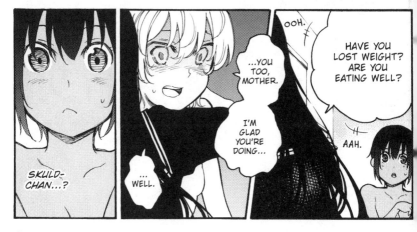

SKULD-CHAN...?

...YOU TOO, MOTHER.

I'M GLAD YOU'RE DOING...

...WELL.

OOH.

HAVE YOU LOST WEIGHT? ARE YOU EATING WELL?

AAH.

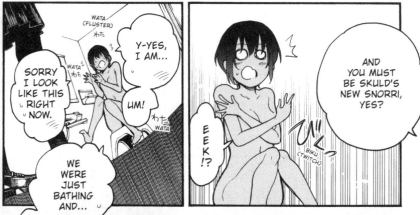

WATA (FLUSTER)

WATA

WATA

SORRY I LOOK LIKE THIS RIGHT NOW.

Y-YES, I AM... UM!

WE WERE JUST BATHING AND...

EEK!?

AND YOU MUST BE SKULD'S NEW SNORRI, YES?

BIKU (TWITCH)

UM...!

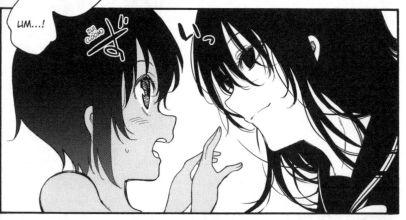

ZUI (CLOSING)

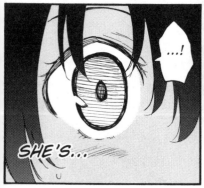

...!

SHE'S...

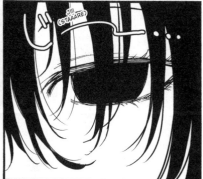

JIII (STAAARE)

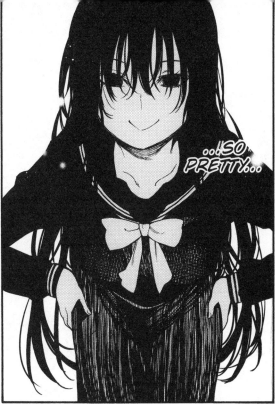

...SO PRETTY...

...LOOK AT YOU, SKULD. ♡

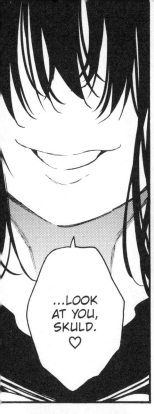

DEFECT...?

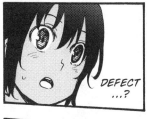

GIRI (GRIT)

WELL, THEN.

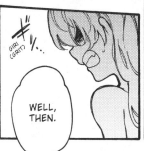

YOU PICKED A NICE BODY TO WORK WITH, UNLIKE THAT **DEFECT** FROM BEFORE. ♡

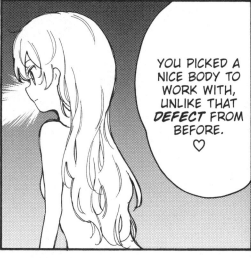

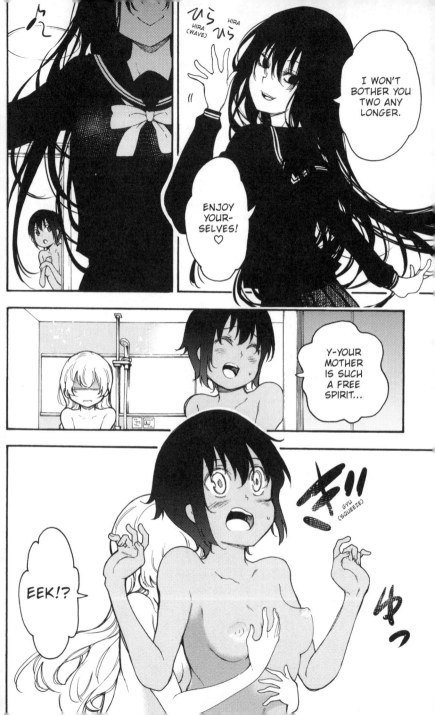

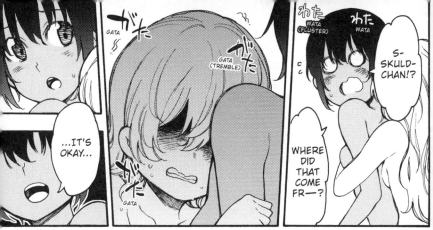

...IT'S OKAY...

GATA

GATA (TREMBLE)

GATA

WATA (FLUSTER)

WATA

S-SKULD-CHAN!?

WHERE DID THAT COME FR—?

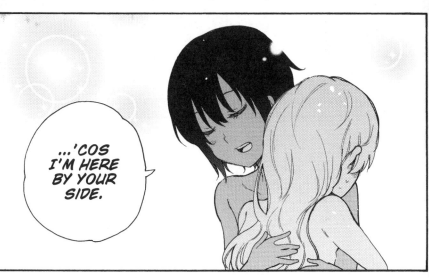

...'COS I'M HERE BY YOUR SIDE.

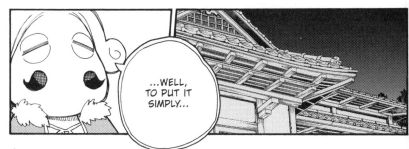

...WELL, TO PUT IT SIMPLY...

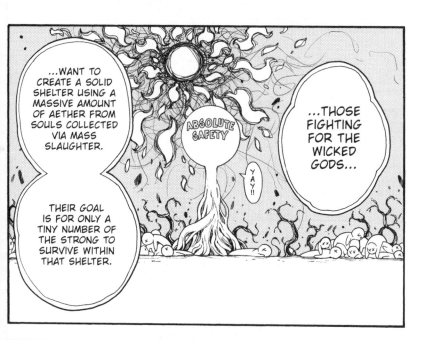

...WANT TO CREATE A SOLID SHELTER USING A MASSIVE AMOUNT OF AETHER FROM SOULS COLLECTED VIA MASS SLAUGHTER.

THEIR GOAL IS FOR ONLY A TINY NUMBER OF THE STRONG TO SURVIVE WITHIN THAT SHELTER.

ABSOLUTE SAFETY

YAY!!

...THOSE FIGHTING FOR THE WICKED GODS...

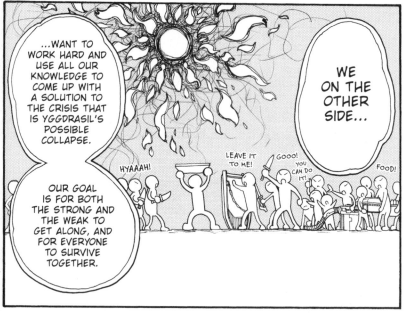

...WANT TO WORK HARD AND USE ALL OUR KNOWLEDGE TO COME UP WITH A SOLUTION TO THE CRISIS THAT IS YGGDRASIL'S POSSIBLE COLLAPSE.

OUR GOAL IS FOR BOTH THE STRONG AND THE WEAK TO GET ALONG, AND FOR EVERYONE TO SURVIVE TOGETHER.

HYAAAH!

LEAVE IT TO ME!

GOOO!

YOU CAN DO IT!

FOOD!

WE ON THE OTHER SIDE...

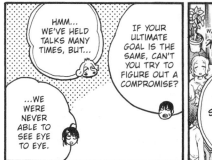

HMM... WE'VE HELD TALKS MANY TIMES, BUT...

IF YOUR ULTIMATE GOAL IS THE SAME, CAN'T YOU TRY TO FIGURE OUT A COMPROMISE?

...WE WERE NEVER ABLE TO SEE EYE TO EYE.

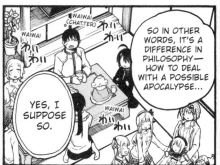

WAIWAI (CHATTER)

WAIWAI

WAIWAI

SO IN OTHER WORDS, IT'S A DIFFERENCE IN PHILOSOPHY— HOW TO DEAL WITH A POSSIBLE APOCALYPSE...

YES, I SUPPOSE SO.

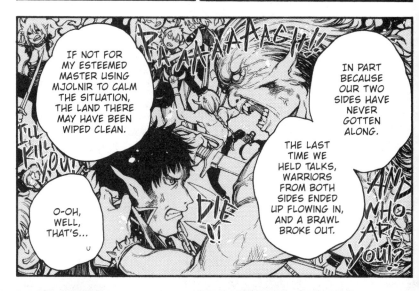

IF NOT FOR MY ESTEEMED MASTER USING MJOLNIR TO CALM THE SITUATION, THE LAND THERE MAY HAVE BEEN WIPED CLEAN.

GRAAAAAAAAGH!!

I'LL KILL YOU!

O-OH, WELL, THAT'S...

DIE!!

IN PART BECAUSE OUR TWO SIDES HAVE NEVER GOTTEN ALONG.

THE LAST TIME WE HELD TALKS, WARRIORS FROM BOTH SIDES ENDED UP FLOWING IN, AND A BRAWL BROKE OUT.

AND WHO ARE YOU?

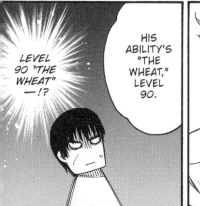

LEVEL 90 "THE WHEAT" —!?

HIS ABILITY'S "THE WHEAT," LEVEL 90.

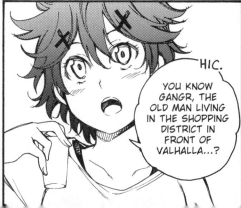

HIC.

YOU KNOW GANGR, THE OLD MAN LIVING IN THE SHOPPING DISTRICT IN FRONT OF VALHALLA...?

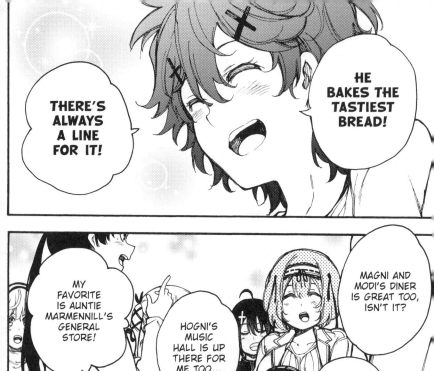

THERE'S ALWAYS A LINE FOR IT!

HE BAKES THE TASTIEST BREAD!

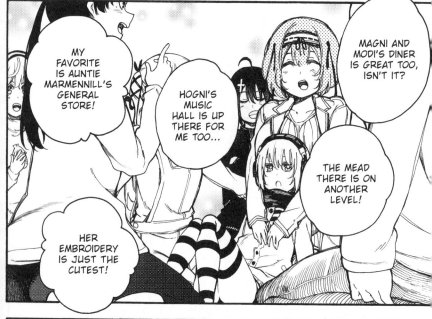

MY FAVORITE IS AUNTIE MARMENNILL'S GENERAL STORE!

HOGNI'S MUSIC HALL IS UP THERE FOR ME TOO...

MAGNI AND MODI'S DINER IS GREAT TOO, ISN'T IT?

THE MEAD THERE IS ON ANOTHER LEVEL!

HER EMBROIDERY IS JUST THE CUTEST!

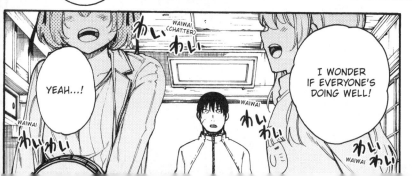

WAIWAI (CHATTER)

わい

YEAH...!

I WONDER IF EVERYONE'S DOING WELL!

WAIWAI

わいわい

わい

WAIWAI

わい わい

WAIWAI

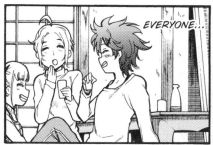

EVERYONE...

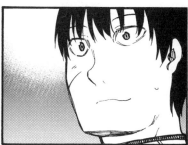

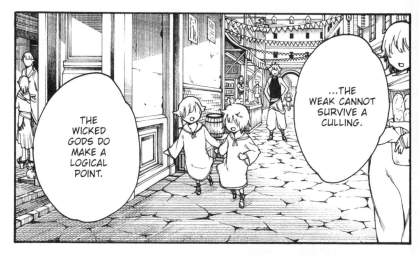

THE WICKED GODS DO MAKE A LOGICAL POINT.

...THE WEAK CANNOT SURVIVE A CULLING.

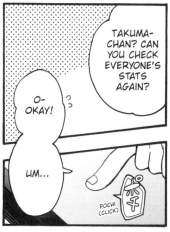

TAKUMA-CHAN? CAN YOU CHECK EVERYONE'S STATS AGAIN?

O-OKAY!

UM...

POCHI (CLICK)

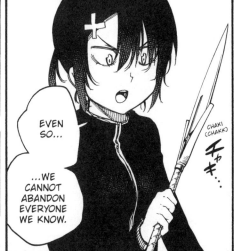

EVEN SO...

...WE CANNOT ABANDON EVERYONE WE KNOW.

CHAKI (CHAKK)

13

SCHWERTLEITE

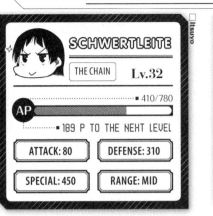

THE CHAIN   **Lv.32**

AP   ■ 410/780

■ 189 P TO THE NEHT LEVEL

ATTACK: 80	DEFENSE: 310
SPECIAL: 450	RANGE: MID

HELMWIGE

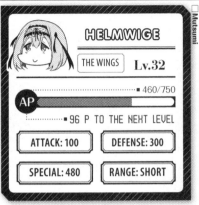

THE WINGS   **Lv.32**

AP   ■ 460/750

■ 96 P TO THE NEHT LEVEL

ATTACK: 100	DEFENSE: 300
SPECIAL: 480	RANGE: SHORT

SIEGRUNE

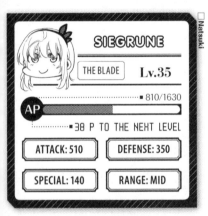

THE BLADE   **Lv.35**

AP   ■ 810/1630

■ 38 P TO THE NEHT LEVEL

ATTACK: 510	DEFENSE: 350
SPECIAL: 140	RANGE: MID

GRIMGERDE

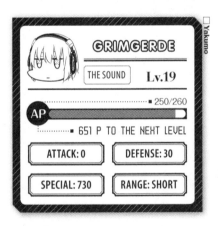

THE SOUND   **Lv.19**

AP   ■ 250/260

■ 651 P TO THE NEHT LEVEL

ATTACK: 0	DEFENSE: 30
SPECIAL: 730	RANGE: SHORT

ROSSWEISSE

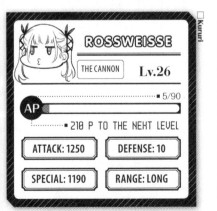

THE CANNON   **Lv.26**

AP   ■ 5/90

■ 210 P TO THE NEHT LEVEL

ATTACK: 1250	DEFENSE: 10
SPECIAL: 1190	RANGE: LONG

EINHERJAR

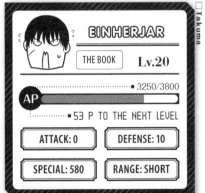

THE BOOK   **Lv.20**

AP   ■ 3250/3800

■ 53 P TO THE NEHT LEVEL

ATTACK: 0	DEFENSE: 10
SPECIAL: 580	RANGE: SHORT

THE 9 VALKYRIE SISTERS: A COMPLETE BREAKDOWN!

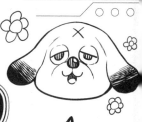

Ver. 2 AWOO!

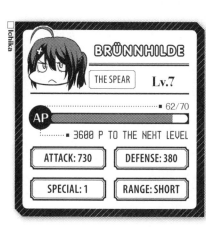

☐ Ichika

BRÜNNHILDE

| THE SPEAR | Lv.7 |

AP ▪ 62/70

▪ 3600 P TO THE NEHT LEVEL

| ATTACK: 730 | DEFENSE: 380 |
| SPECIAL: 1 | RANGE: SHORT |

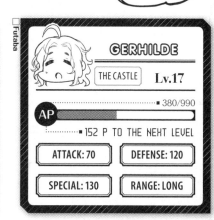

☐ Futaba

GERHILDE

| THE CASTLE | Lv.17 |

AP ▪ 380/990

▪ 152 P TO THE NEHT LEVEL

| ATTACK: 70 | DEFENSE: 120 |
| SPECIAL: 130 | RANGE: LONG |

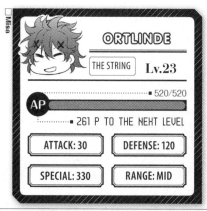

☐ Misa

ORTLINDE

| THE STRING | Lv.23 |

AP ▪ 520/520

▪ 261 P TO THE NEHT LEVEL

| ATTACK: 30 | DEFENSE: 120 |
| SPECIAL: 330 | RANGE: MID |

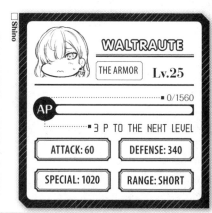

☐ Shino

WALTRAUTE

| THE ARMOR | Lv.25 |

AP ▪ 0/1560

▪ 3 P TO THE NEHT LEVEL

| ATTACK: 60 | DEFENSE: 340 |
| SPECIAL: 1020 | RANGE: SHORT |

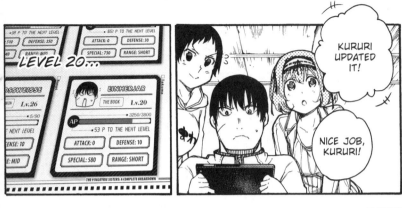
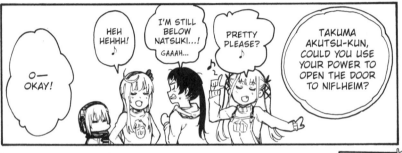
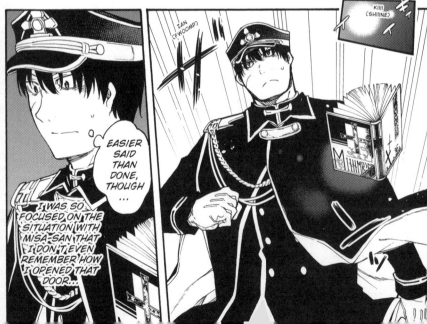

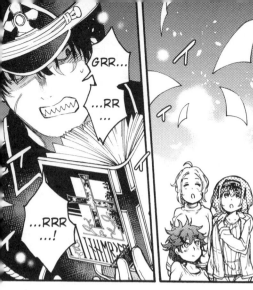

GRR...

...RR...

...RRR...!

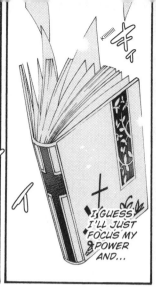

I GUESS I'LL JUST FOCUS MY POWER AND...

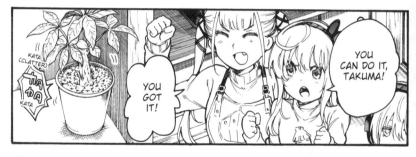

KATA (CLATTER)

KATA

YOU GOT IT!

YOU CAN DO IT, TAKUMA!

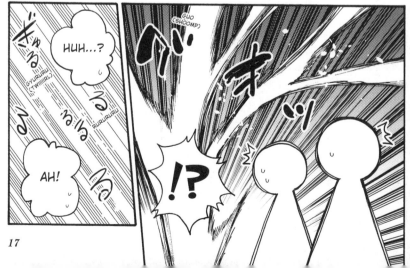

HUH...?

GYURURU (TWIIIRL)

RURURURU

AH!

GUO (SHOOMP)

!?

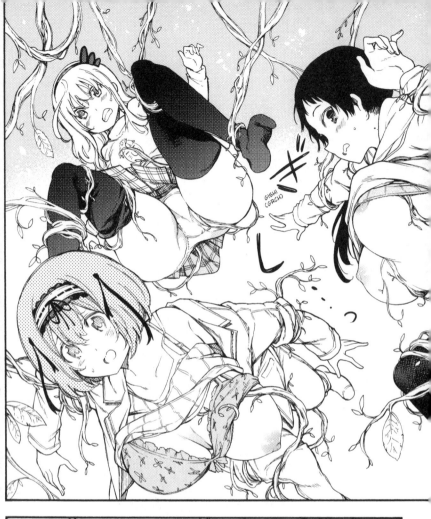

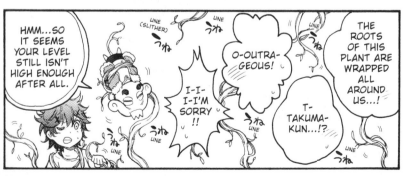

HMM...SO IT SEEMS YOUR LEVEL STILL ISN'T HIGH ENOUGH AFTER ALL.

UNE (SLITHER)

UNE

O-OUTRA-GEOUS!

THE ROOTS OF THIS PLANT ARE WRAPPED ALL AROUND US...!

I-I-I-I'M SORRY!!

T-TAKUMA-KUN...!?

UNE

UNE

UNE

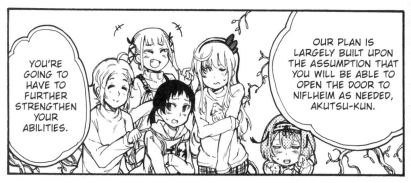

YOU'RE GOING TO HAVE TO FURTHER STRENGTHEN YOUR ABILITIES.

OUR PLAN IS LARGELY BUILT UPON THE ASSUMPTION THAT YOU WILL BE ABLE TO OPEN THE DOOR TO NIFLHEIM AS NEEDED, AKUTSU-KUN.

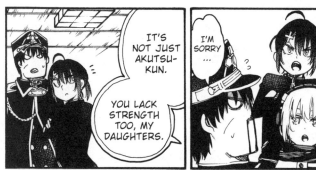

IT'S NOT JUST AKUTSU-KUN.

YOU LACK STRENGTH TOO, MY DAUGHTERS.

I'M SORRY...

THAT'S RIGHT! YOU LACK TRAINING, LOVER!

YOU'RE NO GOOD AT ALL, ONII-CHAN.

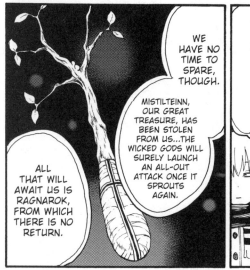

WE HAVE NO TIME TO SPARE, THOUGH.

MISTILTEINN, OUR GREAT TREASURE, HAS BEEN STOLEN FROM US...THE WICKED GODS WILL SURELY LAUNCH AN ALL-OUT ATTACK ONCE IT SPROUTS AGAIN.

ALL THAT WILL AWAIT US IS RAGNAROK, FROM WHICH THERE IS NO RETURN.

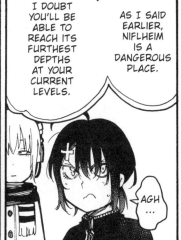

I DOUBT YOU'LL BE ABLE TO REACH ITS FURTHEST DEPTHS AT YOUR CURRENT LEVELS.

AS I SAID EARLIER, NIFLHEIM IS A DANGEROUS PLACE.

AGH...

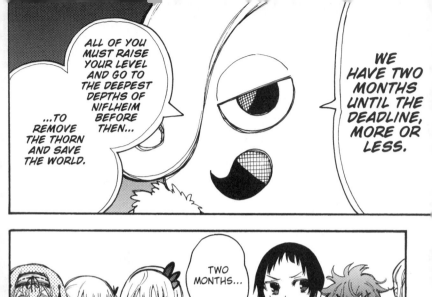

ALL OF YOU MUST RAISE YOUR LEVEL AND GO TO THE DEEPEST DEPTHS OF NIFLHEIM BEFORE THEN...

...TO REMOVE THE THORN AND SAVE THE WORLD.

WE HAVE TWO MONTHS UNTIL THE DEADLINE, MORE OR LESS.

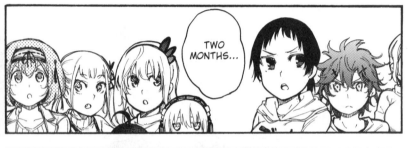

TWO MONTHS...

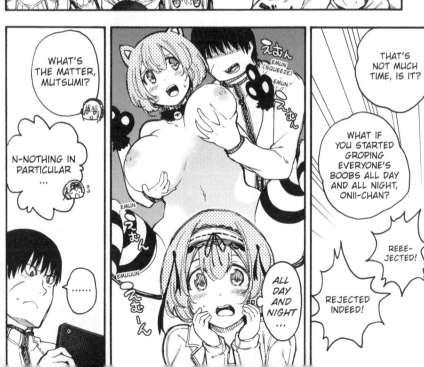

WHAT'S THE MATTER, MUTSUMI?

N-NOTHING IN PARTICULAR...

......

THAT'S NOT MUCH TIME, IS IT?

WHAT IF YOU STARTED GROPING EVERYONE'S BOOBS ALL DAY AND ALL NIGHT, ONII-CHAN?

REEE-JECTED!

REJECTED INDEED!

ALL DAY AND NIGHT...

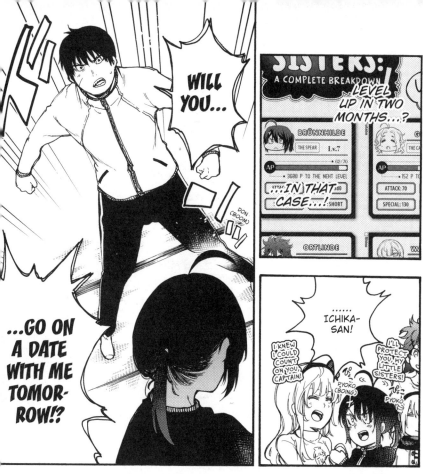

WILL YOU...

...GO ON A DATE WITH ME TOMORROW!?

DON (BOOM)

SISTERS:
A COMPLETE BREAKDOWN

LEVEL UP IN TWO MONTHS...?

BRÜNNHILDE
THE SPEAR   Lv.7

AP   62/70

3600 P TO THE NEXT LEVEL

...IN THAT CASE...! SHORT

ATTACK 580

THE C

AP   152 P T

ATTACK: 70

SPECIAL: 130

ORTLINDE   W

......
ICHIKA-SAN!

I KNEW I COULD COUNT ON YOU, CAPTAIN.

I'LL PROTECT YOU, MY LITTLE SISTERS!

PYOKO (BOING)

PYOKO

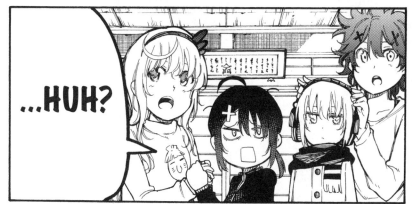

...HUH?

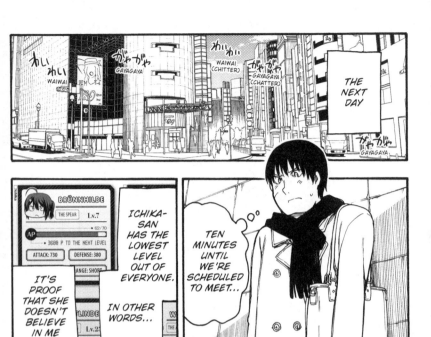

WAIWAI

GAYAGAYA

WAIWAI (CHITTER)

GAYAGAYA (CHATTER)

GAYAGAYA

THE NEXT DAY

BRÜNNHILDE

THE SPEAR   Lv.7

AP   • 62/70

• 3600 P TO THE NEXT LEVEL

ATTACK: 730   DEFENSE: 380

ANGE: SHORT

ICHIKA-SAN HAS THE LOWEST LEVEL OUT OF EVERYONE.

IN OTHER WORDS...

IT'S PROOF THAT SHE DOESN'T BELIEVE IN ME AS HER LOVER ...!

LINDE

Lv.2

• 520

NEHT LEVE

FENSE: 120   ATTACK: 60

TEN MINUTES UNTIL WE'RE SCHEDULED TO MEET...

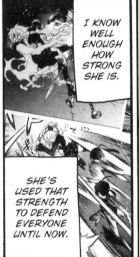

I KNOW WELL ENOUGH HOW STRONG SHE IS.

SHE'S USED THAT STRENGTH TO DEFEND EVERYONE UNTIL NOW.

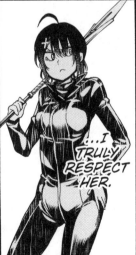

...I TRULY RESPECT HER.

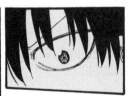

...TO BE HONEST, I WAS AFRAID OF ICHIKA-SAN WHEN WE FIRST MET. I DIDN'T LIKE BEING AROUND HER.

BUT NOW...

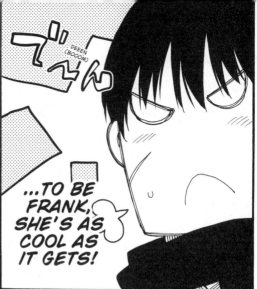

DEEEN (BOOOM)

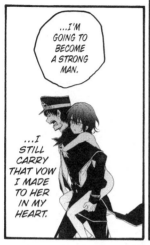

...I'M GOING TO BECOME A STRONG MAN.

...I STILL CARRY THAT VOW I MADE TO HER IN MY HEART.

...TO BE FRANK, SHE'S AS COOL AS IT GETS!

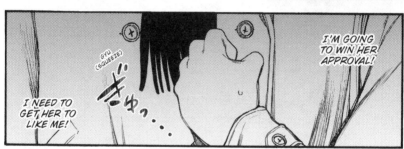

GYU (SQUEEZE)

I'M GOING TO WIN HER APPROVAL!

I NEED TO GET HER TO LIKE ME!

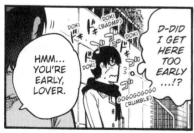

HMM... YOU'RE EARLY, LOVER.

DOKI (BADMP)
DOK!
DOK!

D-DID I GET HERE TOO EARLY ...!?

GOGOGOGOGO (RUMBLE)

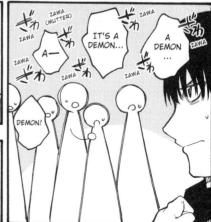

ZAWA (MUTTER)

A—

IT'S A DEMON...

A DEMON ...

ZAWA

DEMON!

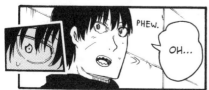

PHEW.

OH...

23

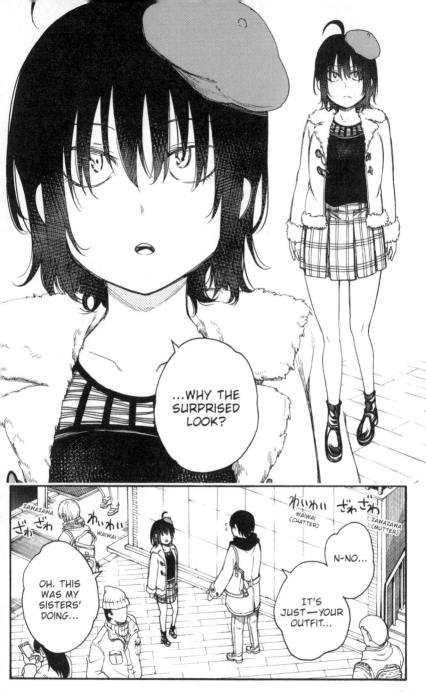

...WHY THE SURPRISED LOOK?

ZAWAZAWA
ざわ ざわ

WAIWAI
わいわい

WAIWAI
(CHATTER)
わいわい

ZAWAZAWA
(MUTTER)
ざわ ざわ

OH. THIS WAS MY SISTERS' DOING...

N-NO...

IT'S JUST—YOUR OUTFIT...

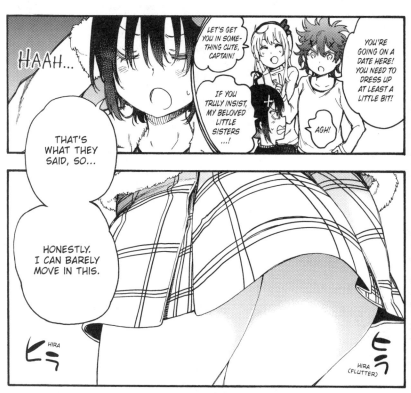

HAAH...

LET'S GET YOU IN SOMETHING CUTE, CAPTAIN!

YOU'RE GOING ON A DATE HERE! YOU NEED TO DRESS UP AT LEAST A LITTLE BIT!

IF YOU TRULY INSIST, MY BELOVED LITTLE SISTERS ...!

AGH!

THAT'S WHAT THEY SAID, SO...

HONESTLY. I CAN BARELY MOVE IN THIS.

HIRA

HIRA (FLUTTER)

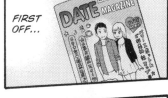

FIRST OFF...

DATE MAGAZINE

U-UM!

... "COMPLIMENT HER OUTFIT"!

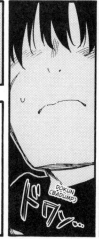

DOKUN (BADUMP)

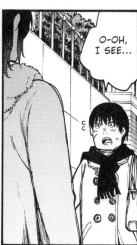

O-OH, I SEE...

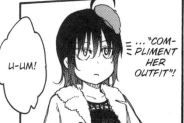

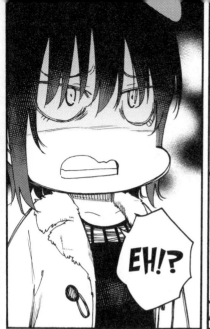

EH!?

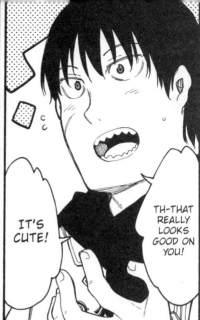

IT'S CUTE!

TH-THAT REALLY LOOKS GOOD ON YOU!

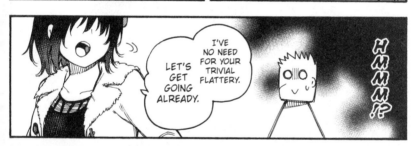

LET'S GET GOING ALREADY.

I'VE NO NEED FOR YOUR TRIVIAL FLATTERY.

HMMM!?

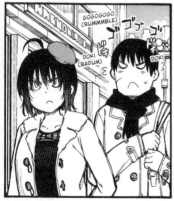

GOGOGOGO (RUMMMBLE)

DOKI (BADUM)

DOKI?

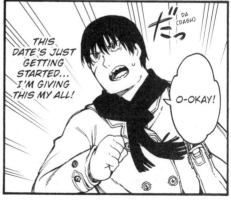

THIS DATE'S JUST GETTING STARTED... I'M GIVING THIS MY ALL!

DA (DASH)

O-OKAY!

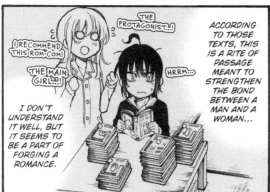

I RECOMMEND THIS ROM-COM!

THE MAIN GIRL...!

THE PROTAGONIST...!

HRRM...

I DON'T UNDERSTAND IT WELL, BUT IT SEEMS TO BE A PART OF FORGING A ROMANCE.

ACCORDING TO THOSE TEXTS, THIS IS A RITE OF PASSAGE MEANT TO STRENGTHEN THE BOND BETWEEN A MAN AND A WOMAN...

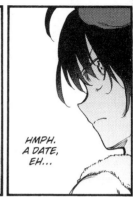

HMPH. A DATE, EH...

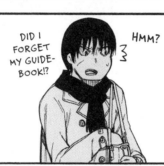

BUT NO... MORE THAN THAT, I APPROVE OF HIS CONCERN FOR MY LITTLE SISTERS!

DID I FORGET MY GUIDE-BOOK!?

HMM?

OUR LOVER DETERMINED THAT WE MUST RAISE THE LEVEL OF OUR ABILITIES IN BATTLE BEFORE WE STORM NIFLHEIM...

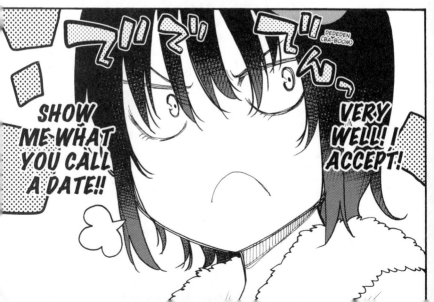

DEDEDEN (BA-BOOM)

SHOW ME WHAT YOU CALL A DATE!!

VERY WELL! I ACCEPT!

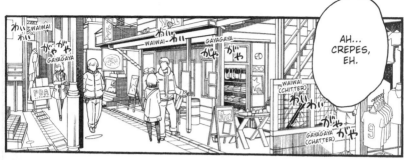

わいWAIWAI
わい
WAIWAI-わい

がやがや
や
GAYAGAYA

わいわい
わい

がやがや
や
GAYAGAYA

WAIWAI
(CHITTER)
わいい
わい

がや
GAYAGAYA
(CHATTER)
がや

AH...
CREPES,
EH.

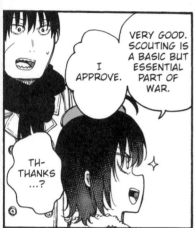

VERY GOOD.
SCOUTING IS
A BASIC BUT
ESSENTIAL
PART OF
WAR.

I
APPROVE.

TH-
THANKS
...?

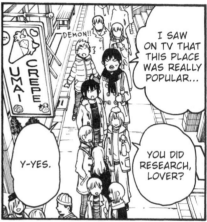

DEMON!!

I SAW
ON TV THAT
THIS PLACE
WAS REALLY
POPULAR...

Y-YES.

YOU DID
RESEARCH,
LOVER?

UMAI

CREPE

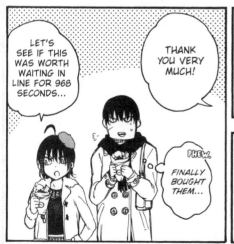

LET'S
SEE IF THIS
WAS WORTH
WAITING IN
LINE FOR 968
SECONDS...

THANK
YOU VERY
MUCH!

PHEW.

FINALLY
BOUGHT
THEM...

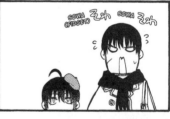

SOWA
(FIDGET) そわ

SOWA
そわ

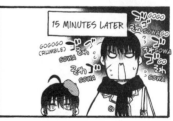

15 MINUTES LATER

ゴゴゴ
GOGOGO
そわ
SOWA

GOGOGO
(RUMBLE)
ゴゴゴ
そわ
そわ

GO

そわ
SOWA

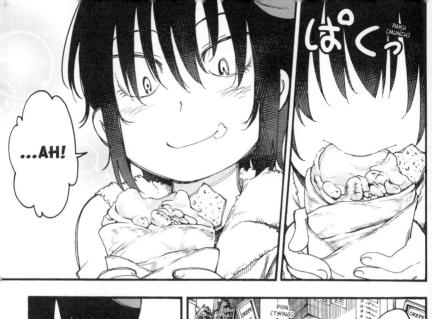

...AH!

PAKU
(MUNCH)

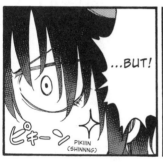

...BUT!

PIKIIIN
(SHINNNG)

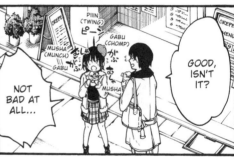

NOT BAD AT ALL...

PIIIN
(TWING)

MUSHA
(MUNCH)

GABU
(CHOMP)

GABU

MUSHA

GOOD, ISN'T IT?

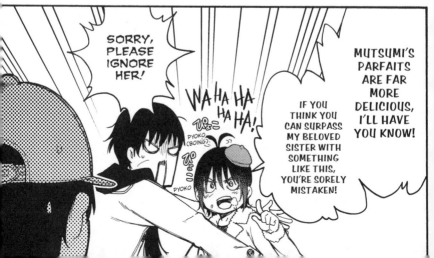

SORRY, PLEASE IGNORE HER!

WA HA HA HA HA!

PYOKO
(BOING)

PYOKO

IF YOU THINK YOU CAN SURPASS MY BELOVED SISTER WITH SOMETHING LIKE THIS, YOU'RE SORELY MISTAKEN!

MUTSUMI'S PARFAITS ARE FAR MORE DELICIOUS, I'LL HAVE YOU KNOW!

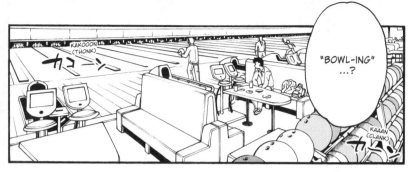

KAKOOON
(THONK)

カコーン

"BOWL-ING"
...?

KAAAN
(CLANK)

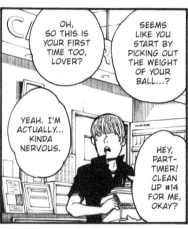

OH, SO THIS IS YOUR FIRST TIME TOO, LOVER?

SEEMS LIKE YOU START BY PICKING OUT THE WEIGHT OF YOUR BALL...?

YEAH. I'M ACTUALLY... KINDA NERVOUS.

HEY, PART-TIMER! CLEAN UP #14 FOR ME, OKAY?

REGISTRATION

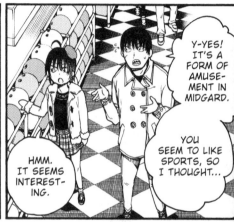

Y-YES! IT'S A FORM OF AMUSE-MENT IN MIDGARD.

YOU SEEM TO LIKE SPORTS, SO I THOUGHT...

HMM. IT SEEMS INTEREST-ING.

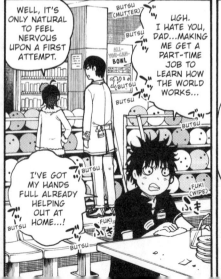

WELL, IT'S ONLY NATURAL TO FEEL NERVOUS UPON A FIRST ATTEMPT.

BUTSU (MUTTER)

BUTSU

ALL-YOU-CAN BOWL

UGH. I HATE YOU, DAD...MAKING ME GET A PART-TIME JOB TO LEARN HOW THE WORLD WORKS...

BUTSU

BUTSU

I'VE GOT MY HANDS FULL ALREADY HELPING OUT AT HOME...!

BUTSU

BUTSU

FUKI (WIPE)

ふき

FUKI

ふき

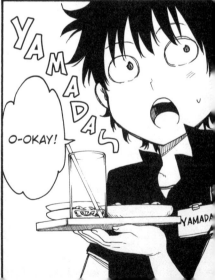

YAMADA

O-OKAY!

YAMADA

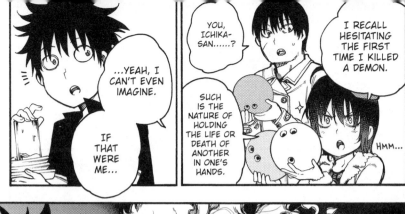

...YEAH, I CAN'T EVEN IMAGINE.

IF THAT WERE ME...

YOU, ICHIKA-SAN......?

SUCH IS THE NATURE OF HOLDING THE LIFE OR DEATH OF ANOTHER IN ONE'S HANDS.

I RECALL HESITATING THE FIRST TIME I KILLED A DEMON.

HMM...

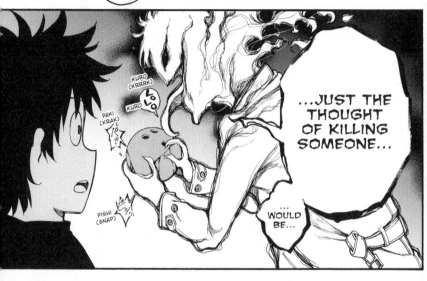

KURO (KRRRK)

KURO

PAKI (KRAK)

PISHI (SNAP)

...JUST THE THOUGHT OF KILLING SOMEONE...

...WOULD BE...

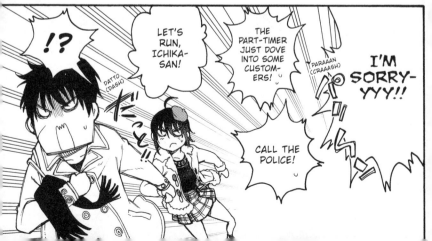

!?

LET'S RUN, ICHIKA-SAN!

DATTO (DASH)

THE PART-TIMER JUST DOVE INTO SOME CUSTOM- ERS!

PARAAAN (CRAAASH)

I'M SORRY-YYY!!

CALL THE POLICE!

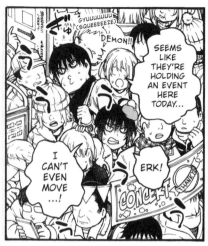

GYUUUUUU (SQUEEEEEZE)

DEMON!!

SEEMS LIKE THEY'RE HOLDING AN EVENT HERE TODAY...

I CAN'T EVEN MOVE ...!

ERK!

CONCERT

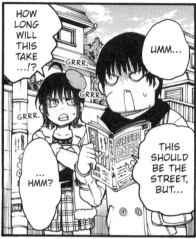

HOW LONG WILL THIS TAKE ...!?

GRRR.

GRRR.

GRRR.

UMM...

... HMM?

SUREFIRE DATES

THIS SHOULD BE THE STREET, BUT...

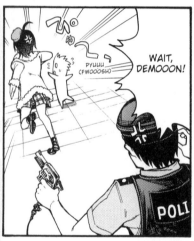

PYUUU (FWOOOSH)

WAIT, DEMOOON!

POLI

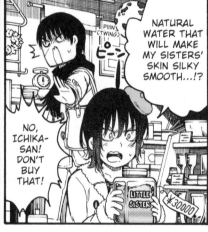

PIIIN (TWING)

NATURAL WATER THAT WILL MAKE MY SISTERS' SKIN SILKY SMOOTH...!?

NO, ICHIKA-SAN! DON'T BUY THAT!

LITTLE SISTER

¥30000

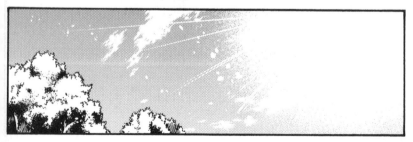

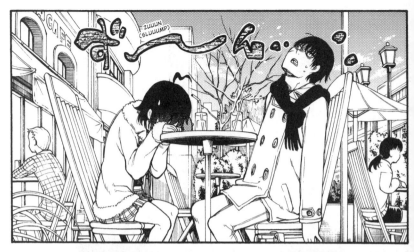

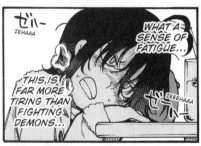

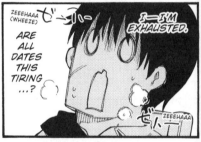

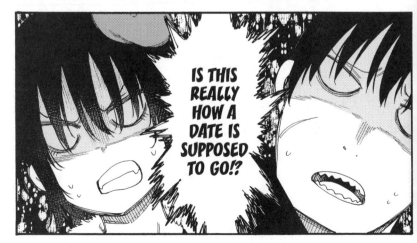

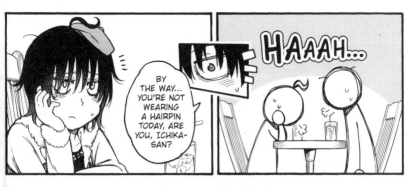

BY THE WAY... YOU'RE NOT WEARING A HAIRPIN TODAY, ARE YOU, ICHIKA-SAN?

HAAAH...

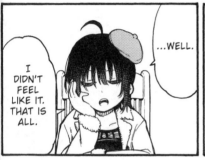

...WELL.

I DIDN'T FEEL LIKE IT. THAT IS ALL.

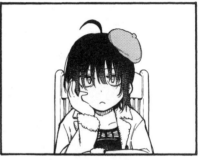

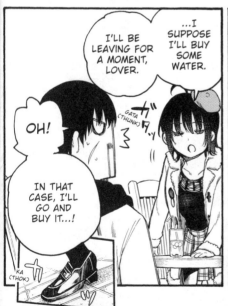

I'LL BE LEAVING FOR A MOMENT, LOVER.

...I SUPPOSE I'LL BUY SOME WATER.

OH!

IN THAT CASE, I'LL GO AND BUY IT...!

GATA (*THUNK*)

KA (*THOK*)

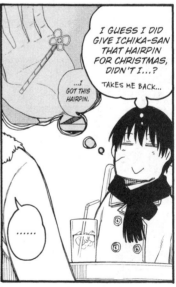

I GUESS I DID GIVE ICHIKA-SAN THAT HAIRPIN FOR CHRISTMAS, DIDN'T I...?

TAKES ME BACK...

...I GOT THIS HAIRPIN.

......

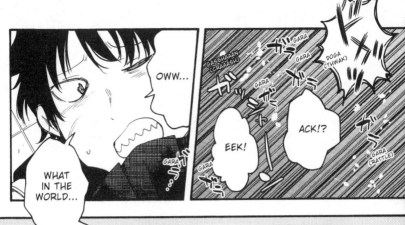

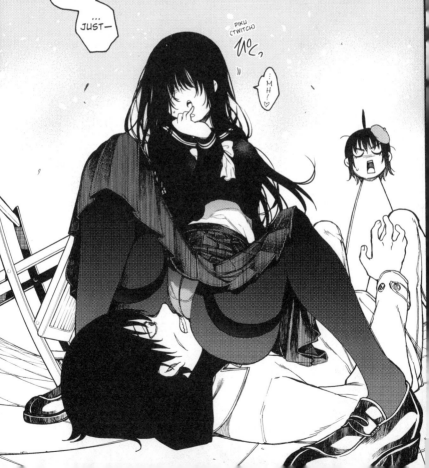

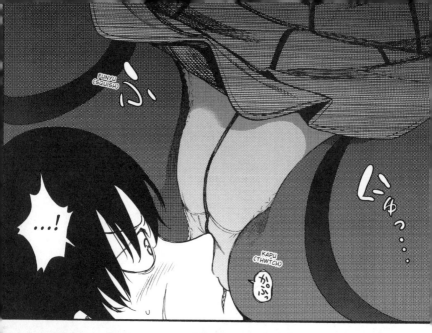

FUNYU (SQUISH)

KAPU (THWTCH)

...!

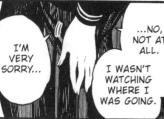

I'M VERY SORRY...

...NO, NOT AT ALL.

I WASN'T WATCHING WHERE I WAS GOING.

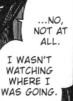

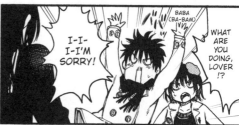

BABA (BA-BAM)

I-I-I-I'M SORRY!

WHAT ARE YOU DOING, LOVER!?

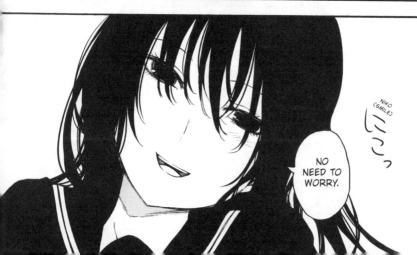

NIKO (SMILE)

NO NEED TO WORRY.

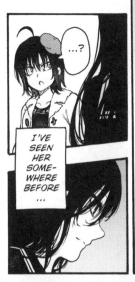

...?

I'VE SEEN HER SOME- WHERE BEFORE...

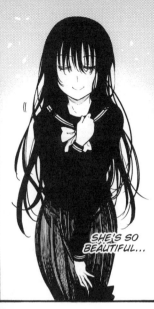

SHE'S SO BEAUTIFUL...

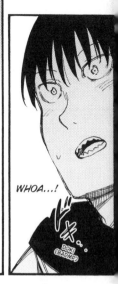

WHOA...!

DOKI (BADMP)

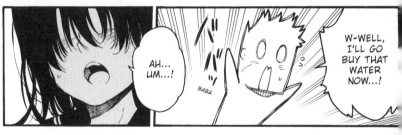

AH... UM...!

BABA

W-WELL, I'LL GO BUY THAT WATER NOW...!

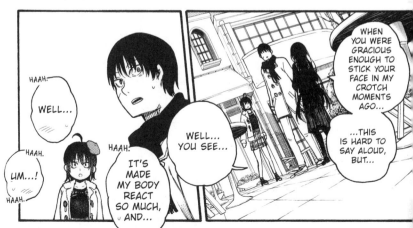

HAAH.

WELL...

HAAH.

UM...!

HAAH.

HAAH.

WELL... YOU SEE...

IT'S MADE MY BODY REACT SO MUCH, AND...

WHEN YOU WERE GRACIOUS ENOUGH TO STICK YOUR FACE IN MY CROTCH MOMENTS AGO...

...THIS IS HARD TO SAY ALOUD, BUT...

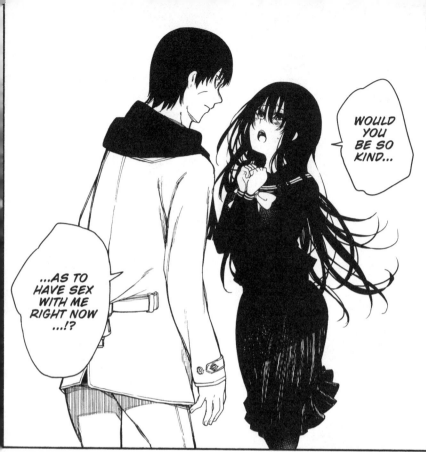

WOULD YOU BE SO KIND...

...AS TO HAVE SEX WITH ME RIGHT NOW ...!?

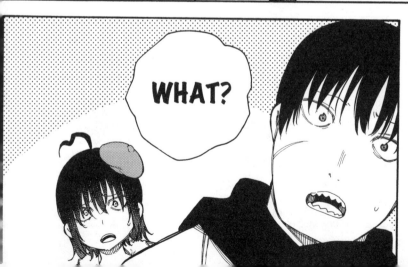

WHAT?

Chapter 56: The Declaring Lover

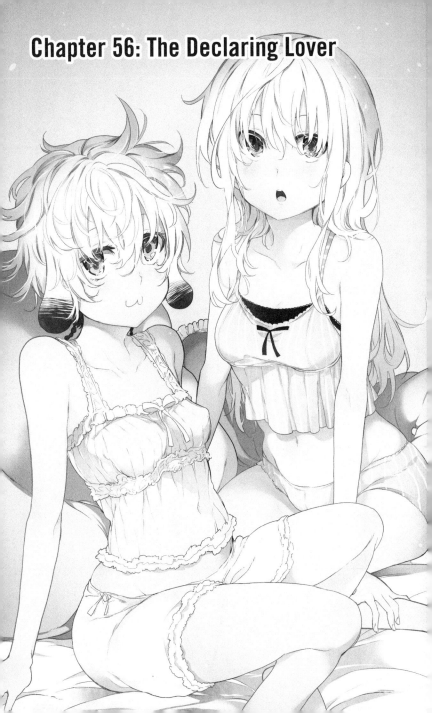

Val X Love

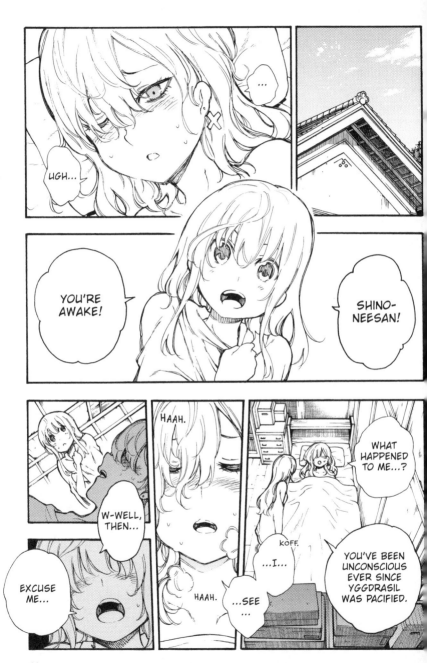

UGH...

...

YOU'RE AWAKE!

SHINO-NEESAN!

HAAH.

W-WELL, THEN...

EXCUSE ME...

HAAH.

...I...

...SEE...

KOFF.

WHAT HAPPENED TO ME...?

YOU'VE BEEN UNCONSCIOUS EVER SINCE YGGDRASIL WAS PACIFIED.

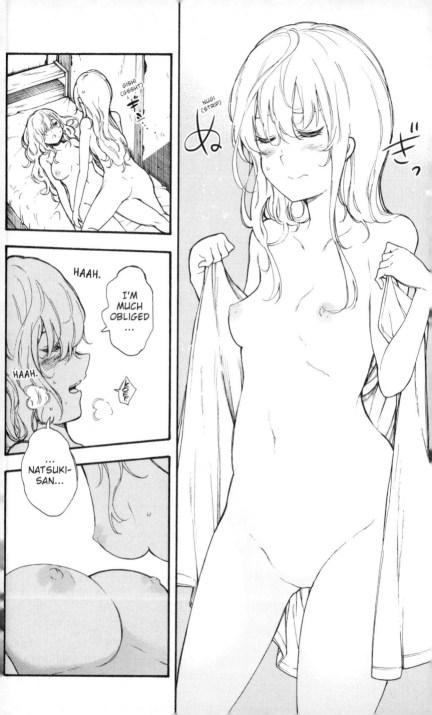

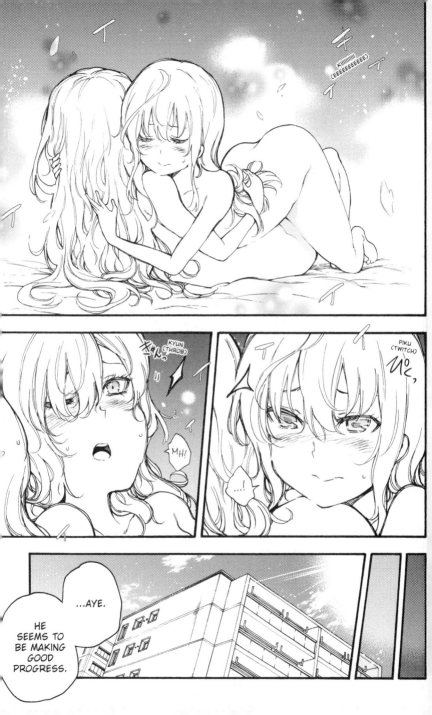

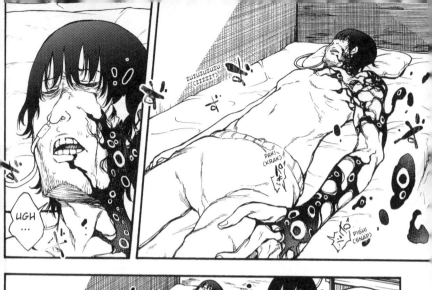

UGH
...

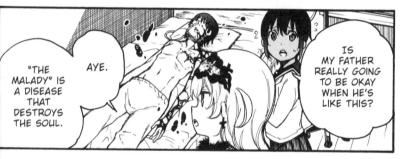

"THE MALADY" IS A DISEASE THAT DESTROYS THE SOUL.

AYE.

IS MY FATHER REALLY GOING TO BE OKAY WHEN HE'S LIKE THIS?

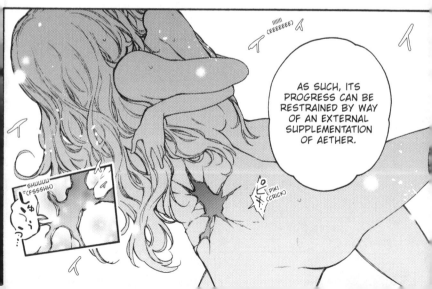

AS SUCH, ITS PROGRESS CAN BE RESTRAINED BY WAY OF AN EXTERNAL SUPPLEMENTATION OF AETHER.

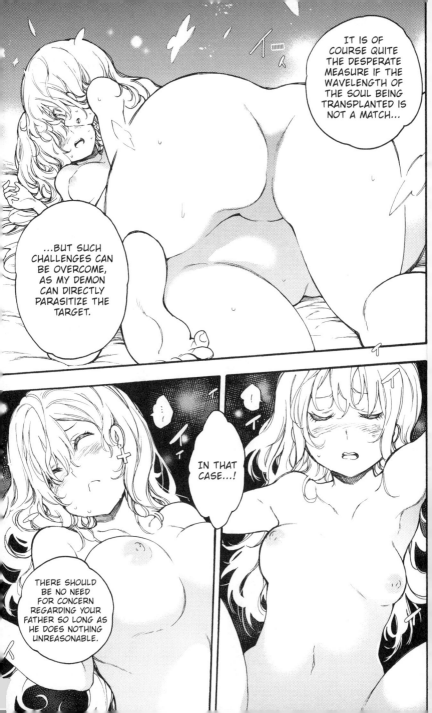

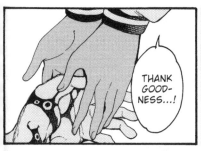

THANK GOOD-NESS...!

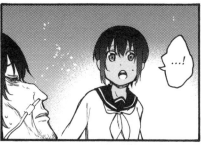

...!

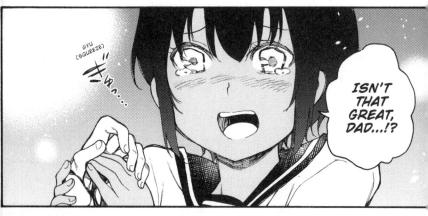

GYU
(SQUEEZE)

ISN'T THAT GREAT, DAD...!?

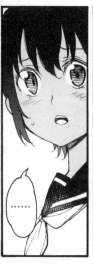

......

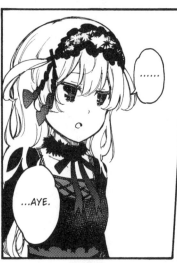

......

...AYE.

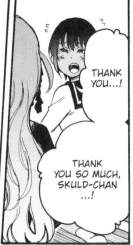

THANK YOU...!

THANK YOU SO MUCH, SKULD-CHAN...!

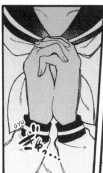

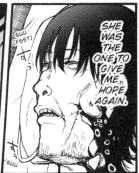

SHE WAS THE ONE TO GIVE ME HOPE AGAIN.

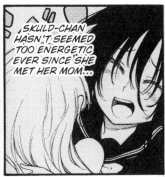

SKULD-CHAN HASN'T SEEMED TOO ENERGETIC EVER SINCE SHE MET HER MOM...

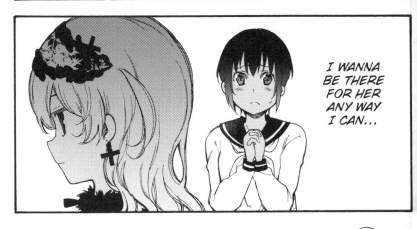

I WANNA BE THERE FOR HER ANY WAY I CAN...

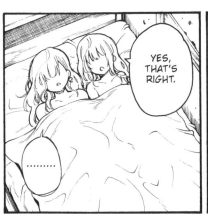

YES, THAT'S RIGHT.

....

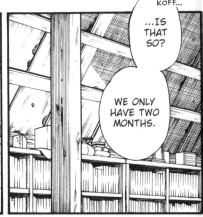

KOFF...

...IS THAT SO?

WE ONLY HAVE TWO MONTHS.

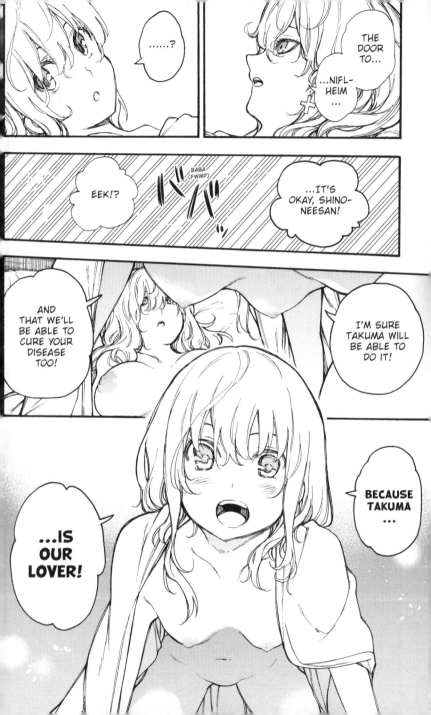

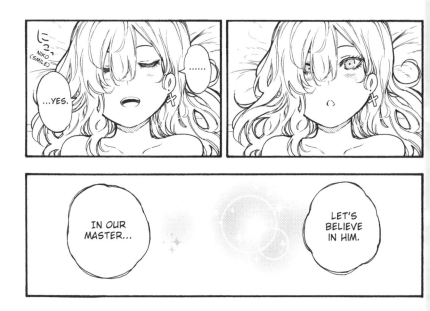

NIKO
(SMILE)

...YES.

......

IN OUR MASTER...

LET'S BELIEVE IN HIM.

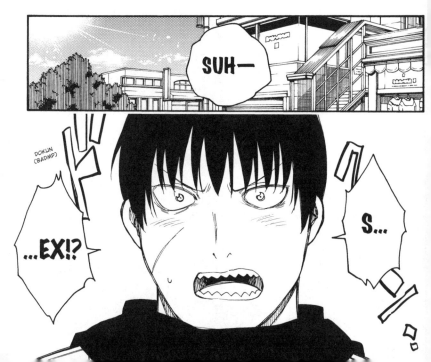

SUH—

DOKUN
(BADMP)

...EX!?

S...

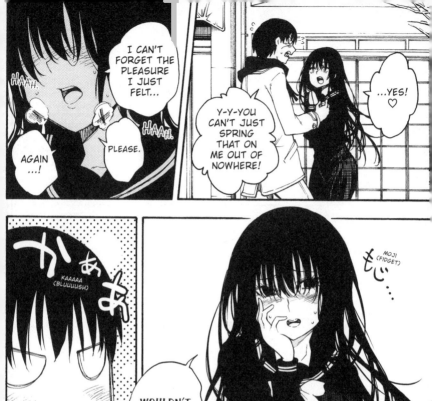
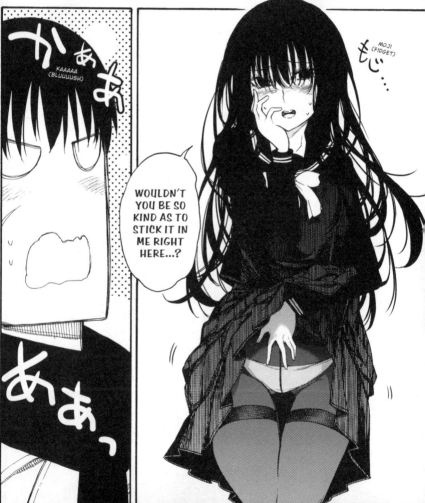

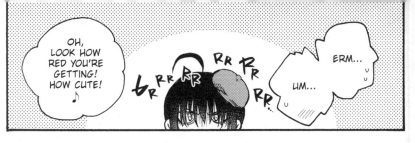

OH, LOOK HOW RED YOU'RE GETTING! HOW CUTE! ♪

ERM...

UM...

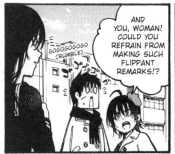

AND YOU, WOMAN! COULD YOU REFRAIN FROM MAKING SUCH FLIPPANT REMARKS!?

GOGOGOGOGO (RUMBLE)

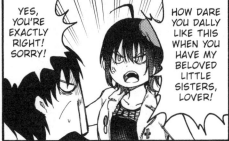

YES, YOU'RE EXACTLY RIGHT! SORRY!

HOW DARE YOU DALLY LIKE THIS WHEN YOU HAVE MY BELOVED LITTLE SISTERS, LOVER!

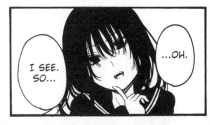

I SEE. SO...

...OH.

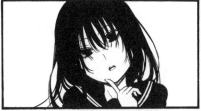

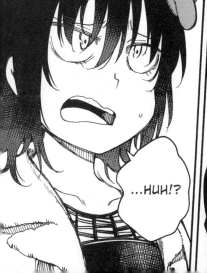

...HUH!?

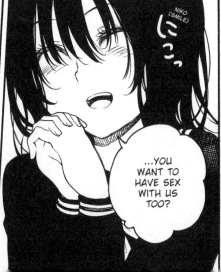

NIKO (SMILE)

...YOU WANT TO HAVE SEX WITH US TOO?

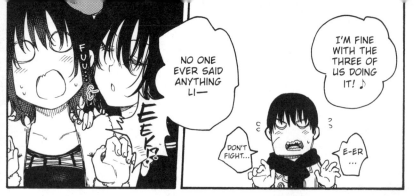

FUU...

EEK!!

NO ONE EVER SAID ANYTHING LI—

I'M FINE WITH THE THREE OF US DOING IT! ♪

DON'T FIGHT...

E-ER...

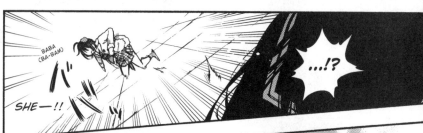

BABA (BA-BAM)

SHE—!!

...!?

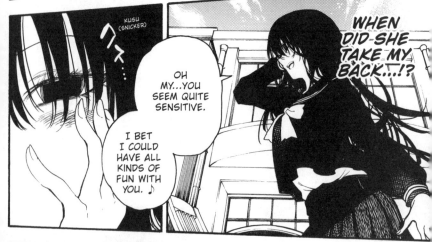

KUSU (SNICKER)

OH MY...YOU SEEM QUITE SENSITIVE.

I BET I COULD HAVE ALL KINDS OF FUN WITH YOU. ♪

WHEN DID SHE TAKE MY BACK...!?

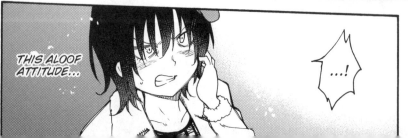

THIS ALOOF ATTITUDE...

...!

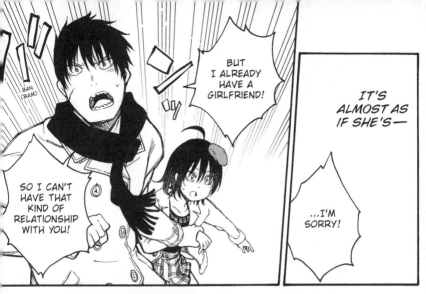

BAN
(BAM)

BUT I ALREADY HAVE A GIRLFRIEND!

SO I CAN'T HAVE THAT KIND OF RELATIONSHIP WITH YOU!

IT'S ALMOST AS IF SHE'S—

...I'M SORRY!

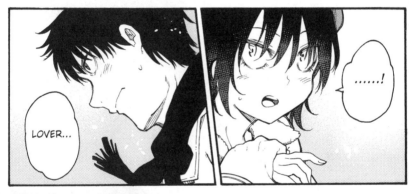

......!

LOVER...

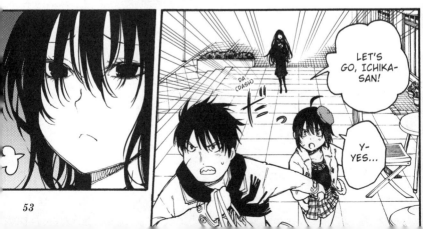

LET'S GO, ICHIKA-SAN!

DA
(DASH)

Y-YES...

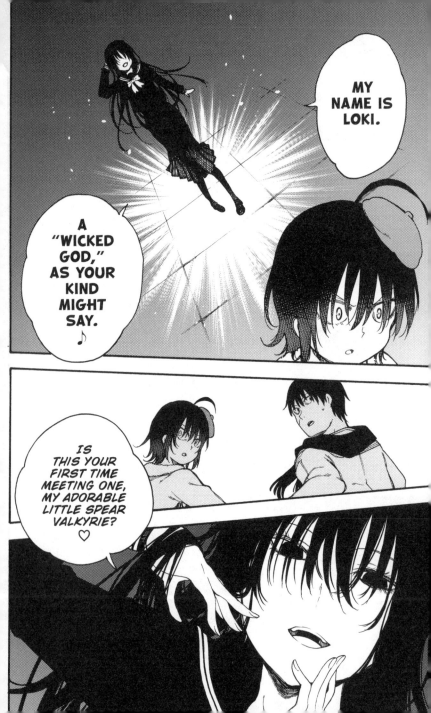

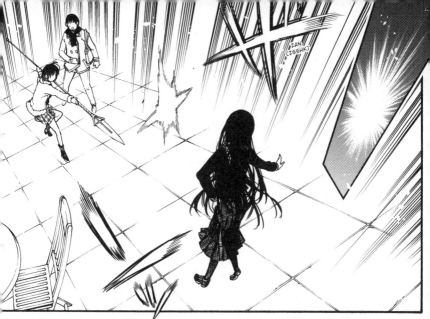

ZAN
(ZSSHK)

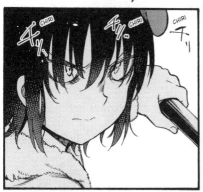

CHIRI
CHIRI
CHIRI
チ

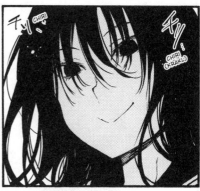

チ CHIRI
チ
CHIRI
(KRAK)

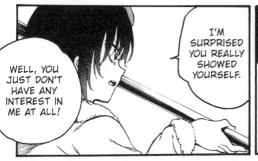

WELL, YOU JUST DON'T HAVE ANY INTEREST IN ME AT ALL!

I'M SURPRISED YOU REALLY SHOWED YOURSELF.

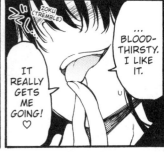

ZOKU
(TREMBLE)

IT REALLY GETS ME GOING! ♡

...BLOOD-THIRSTY. I LIKE IT.

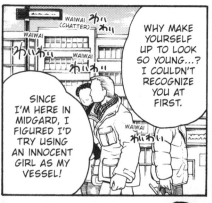

WHY MAKE YOURSELF UP TO LOOK SO YOUNG...? I COULDN'T RECOGNIZE YOU AT FIRST.

SINCE I'M HERE IN MIDGARD, I FIGURED I'D TRY USING AN INNOCENT GIRL AS MY VESSEL!

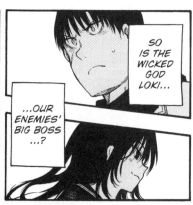

SO IS THE WICKED GOD LOKI...

...OUR ENEMIES' BIG BOSS ...?

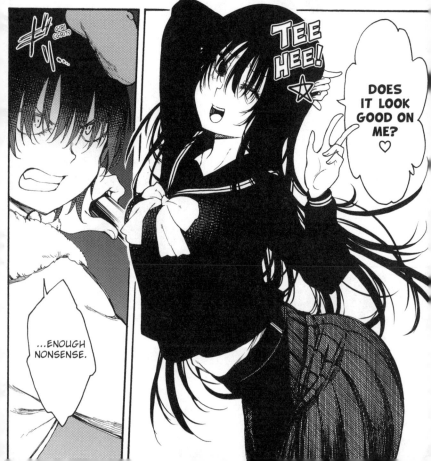

TEE HEE!

DOES IT LOOK GOOD ON ME? ♡

...ENOUGH NONSENSE.

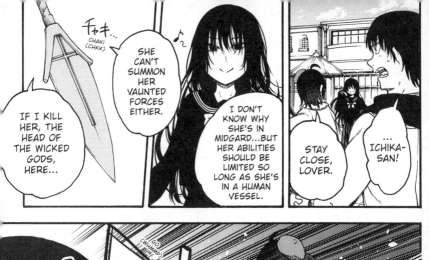

チャキ…
(CHAKI)
(CHHK)

IF I KILL HER, THE HEAD OF THE WICKED GODS, HERE...

SHE CAN'T SUMMON HER VAUNTED FORCES EITHER.

I DON'T KNOW WHY SHE'S IN MIDGARD...BUT HER ABILITIES SHOULD BE LIMITED SO LONG AS SHE'S IN A HUMAN VESSEL.

STAY CLOSE, LOVER.

...ICHIKA-SAN!

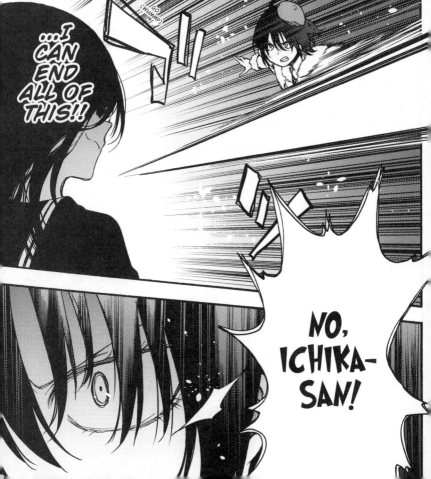

...I CAN END ALL OF THIS!!

ゴ
(GO)
(WHMMP)

NO, ICHIKA-SAN!

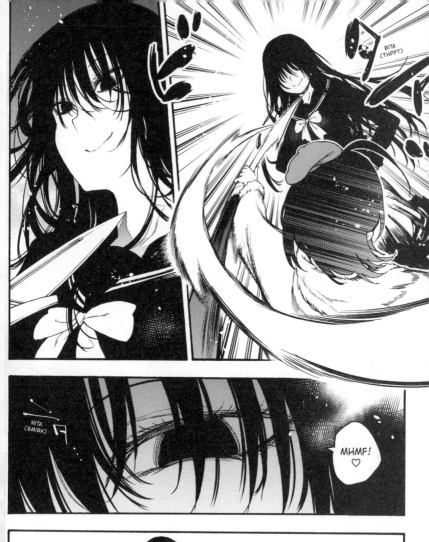

BITA
(THPPT)

NITA
(SMIRK)

MHMF!
♡

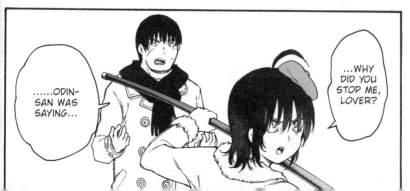

......ODIN-
SAN WAS
SAYING...

...WHY
DID YOU
STOP ME,
LOVER?

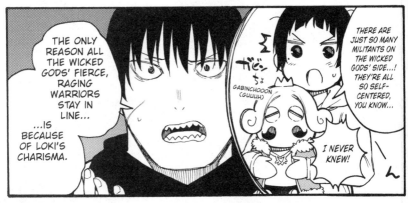

THE ONLY REASON ALL THE WICKED GODS' FIERCE, RAGING WARRIORS STAY IN LINE...

...IS BECAUSE OF LOKI'S CHARISMA.

THERE ARE JUST SO MANY MILITANTS ON THE WICKED GODS' SIDE...! THEY'RE ALL SO SELF-CENTERED, YOU KNOW...

I NEVER KNEW!

GABINCHOOON (GUUUH)

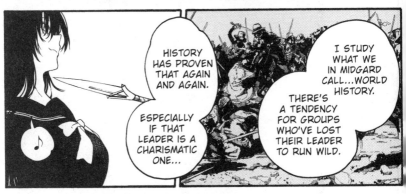

HISTORY HAS PROVEN THAT AGAIN AND AGAIN.

ESPECIALLY IF THAT LEADER IS A CHARISMATIC ONE...

I STUDY WHAT WE IN MIDGARD CALL...WORLD HISTORY.

THERE'S A TENDENCY FOR GROUPS WHO'VE LOST THEIR LEADER TO RUN WILD.

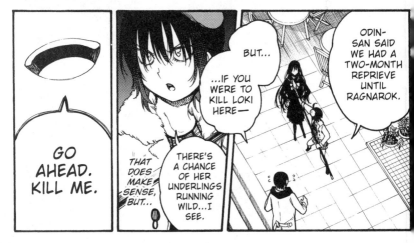

GO AHEAD. KILL ME.

BUT...

...IF YOU WERE TO KILL LOKI HERE—

THAT DOES MAKE SENSE, BUT...

THERE'S A CHANCE OF HER UNDERLINGS RUNNING WILD...I SEE.

ODIN-SAN SAID WE HAD A TWO-MONTH REPRIEVE UNTIL RAGNAROK.

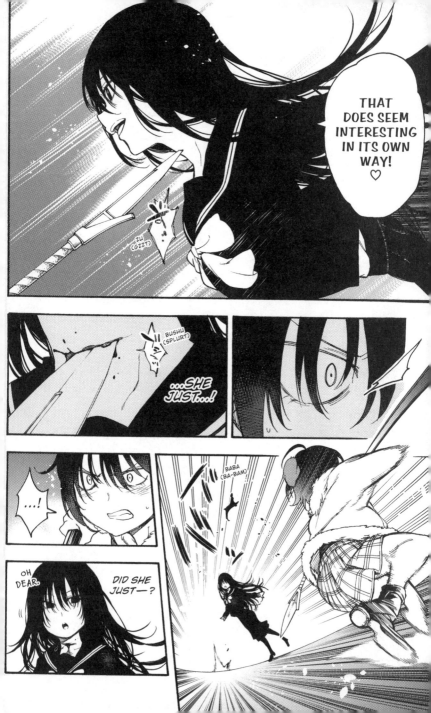

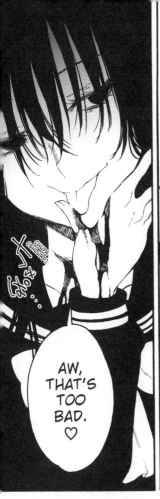

I'M CERTAIN SHE TRIED TO DIE JUST NOW!

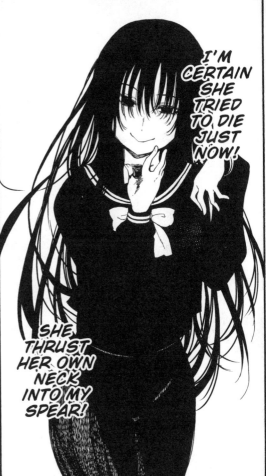

SHE THRUST HER OWN NECK INTO MY SPEAR!

AW, THAT'S TOO BAD. ♡

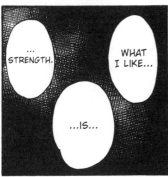

...STRENGTH.

WHAT I LIKE...

...IS...

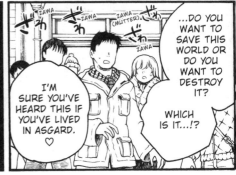

...DO YOU WANT TO SAVE THIS WORLD OR DO YOU WANT TO DESTROY IT?

WHICH IS IT...!?

I'M SURE YOU'VE HEARD THIS IF YOU'VE LIVED IN ASGARD. ♡

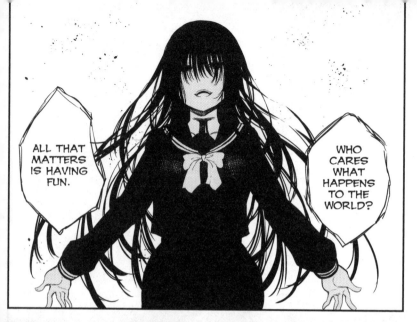

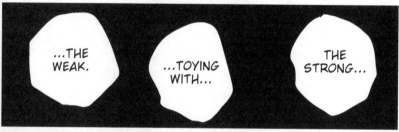

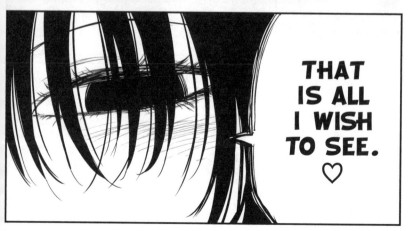

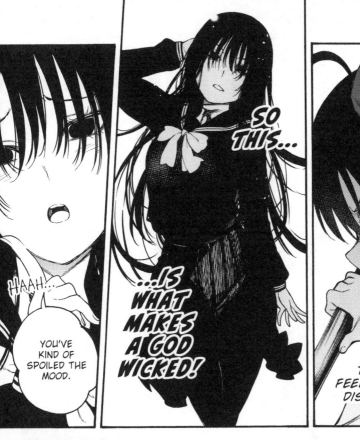

SO THIS...

...IS WHAT MAKES A GOD WICKED!

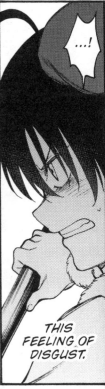

...!

THIS FEELING OF DISGUST.

HAAH!...

YOU'VE KIND OF SPOILED THE MOOD.

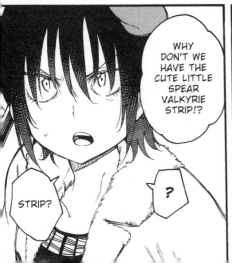

WHY DON'T WE HAVE THE CUTE LITTLE SPEAR VALKYRIE STRIP!?

STRIP?

?

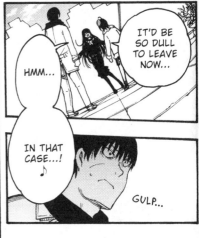

HMM...

IT'D BE SO DULL TO LEAVE NOW...

IN THAT CASE...! ♪

GULP...

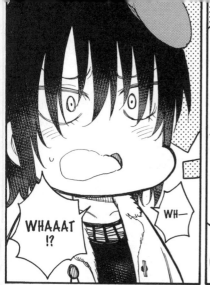

WHAAAT!?

WH—

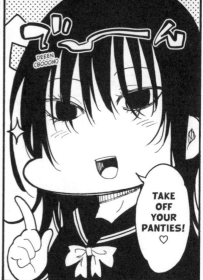

DEEEN (BOOOM)

TAKE OFF YOUR PANTIES! ♡

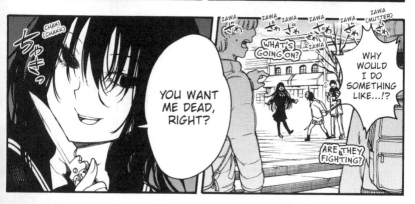

CHAKI (CHAKK)

YOU WANT ME DEAD, RIGHT?

ZAWA ZAWA ZAWA ZAWA ZAWA ZAWA (MUTTER)

WHAT'S GOING ON?

WHY WOULD I DO SOMETHING LIKE...!?

ARE THEY FIGHTING?

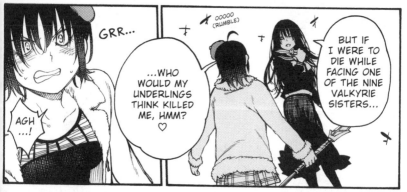

GRR...

AGH...!

...WHO WOULD MY UNDERLINGS THINK KILLED ME, HMM? ♡

OOOOO (RUMBLE)

BUT IF I WERE TO DIE WHILE FACING ONE OF THE NINE VALKYRIE SISTERS...

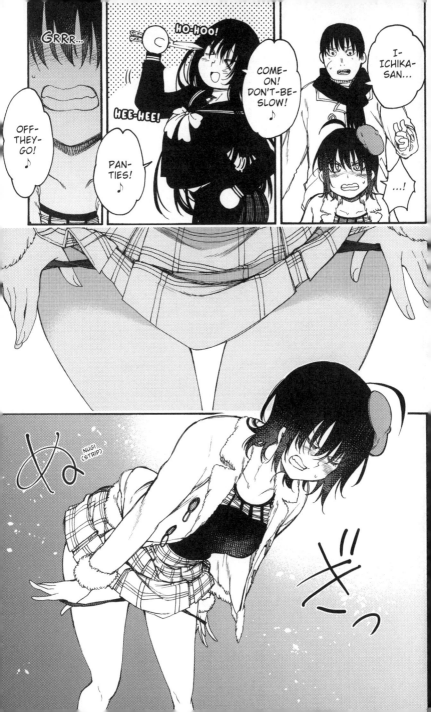

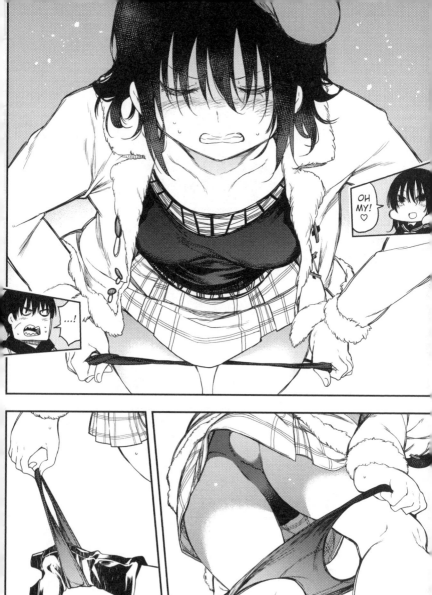
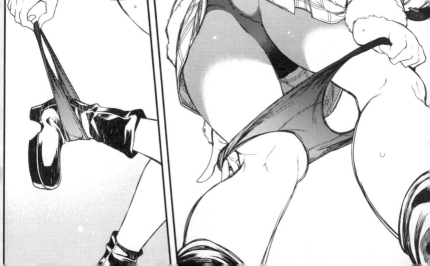

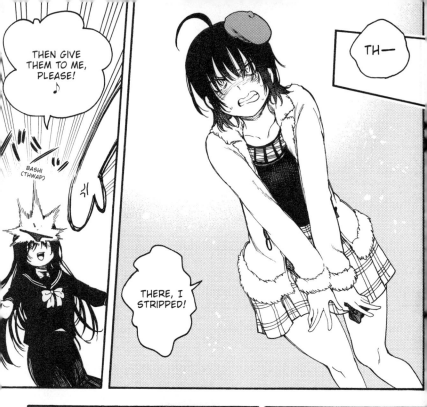

THEN GIVE THEM TO ME, PLEASE! ♪

TH—

BASHI (THWAP)

THERE, I STRIPPED!

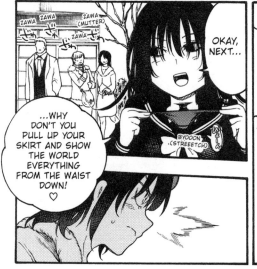

ZAWA ZAWA ZAWA (MUTTER) ZAWA—

OKAY, NEXT...

...WHY DON'T YOU PULL UP YOUR SKIRT AND SHOW THE WORLD EVERYTHING FROM THE WAIST DOWN! ♡

BYOOON (STREEETCH)

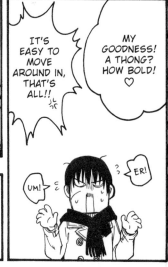

IT'S EASY TO MOVE AROUND IN, THAT'S ALL!!

MY GOODNESS! A THONG? HOW BOLD! ♡

UM!

ER!

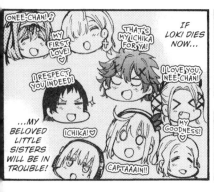

ONEE-CHAN! ♪

MY FIRST LOVE!

THAT'S MY ICHIKA FOR YA!

I RESPECT YOU INDEED!

I LOVE YOU, NEE-CHAN!

...MY BELOVED LITTLE SISTERS WILL BE IN TROUBLE!

ICHIKA! ♡

MY GOODNESS!

CAPTAAAIN!!

IF LOKI DIES NOW...

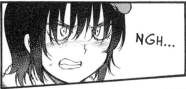

NGH...

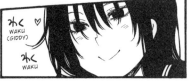

わく
WAKU
(GIDDY)

わく
WAKU

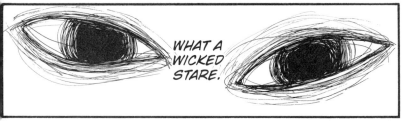

WHAT A WICKED STARE.

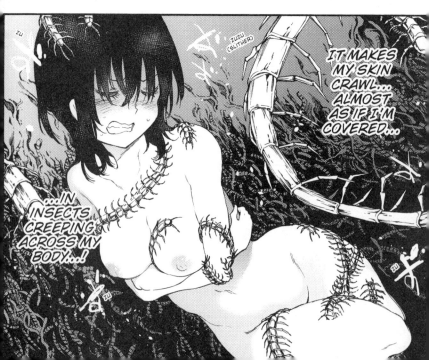

ZU

ズズ
ZUZU
(SLITHER)

IT MAKES MY SKIN CRAWL... ALMOST AS IF I'M COVERED...

...IN INSECTS CREEPING ACROSS MY BODY...!

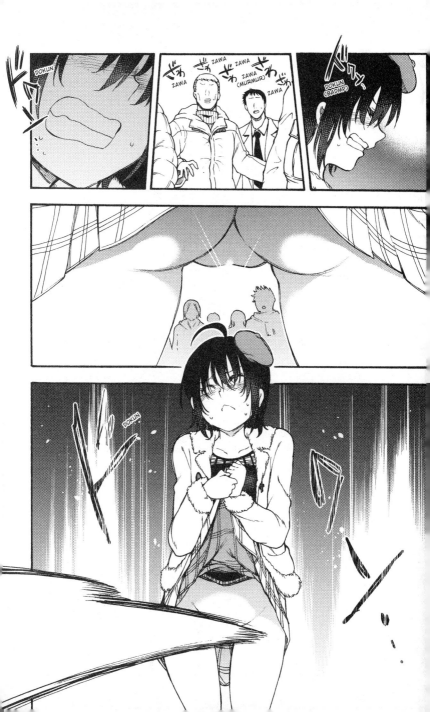

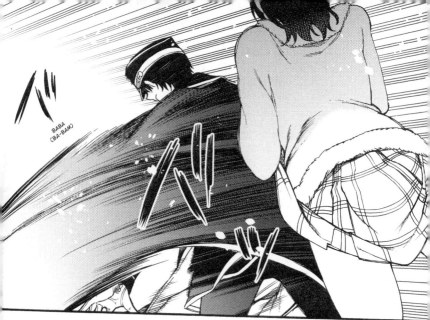

BABA
(BA-BAM)

ヘ゛

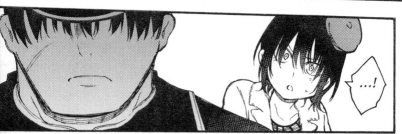

....!

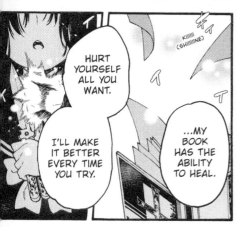

KIIIIII
(SHIIIIINE)

HURT YOURSELF ALL YOU WANT.

I'LL MAKE IT BETTER EVERY TIME YOU TRY.

...MY BOOK HAS THE ABILITY TO HEAL.

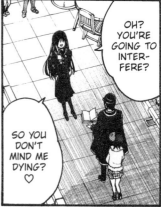

OH? YOU'RE GOING TO INTER-FERE?

SO YOU DON'T MIND ME DYING? ♡

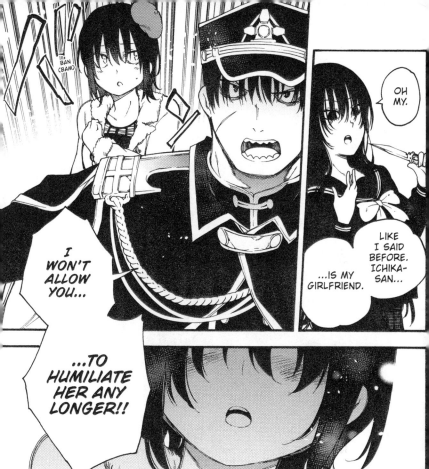

BAM
(BAN)

OH MY.

I WON'T ALLOW YOU...

...IS MY GIRLFRIEND.

LIKE I SAID BEFORE. ICHIKA-SAN...

...TO HUMILIATE HER ANY LONGER!!

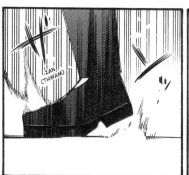

ZAN
(THWAN)

I'M MAKING A DECLARATION HERE AND NOW.

...AND ALSO.

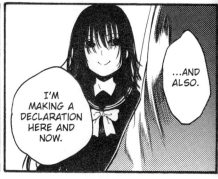

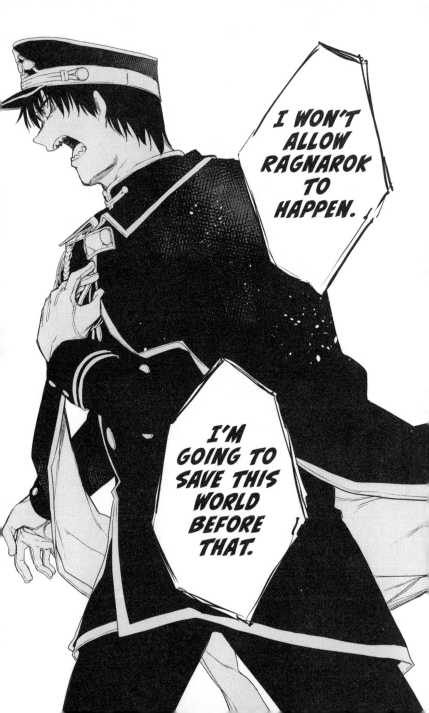

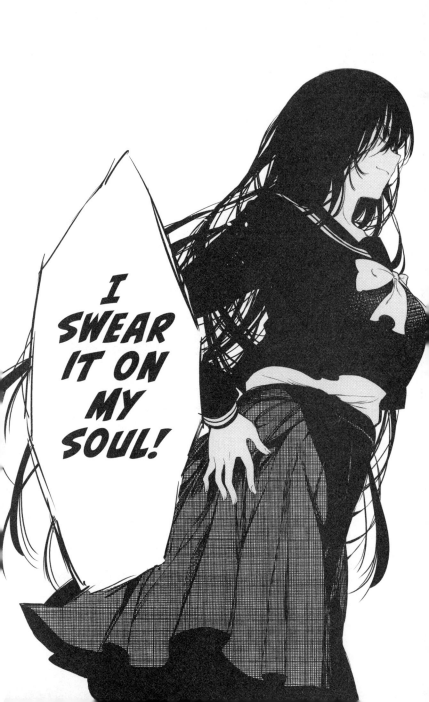

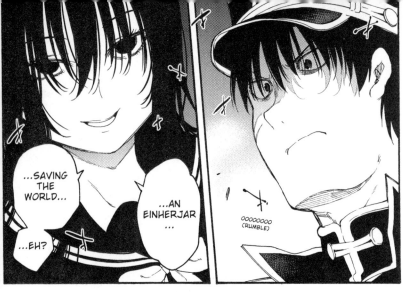

...SAVING THE WORLD...

...EH?

...AN EINHERJAR...

OOOOOOOO (RUMBLE)

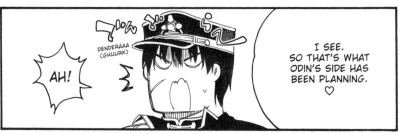

AH!

DENDERAAA (GHUURK)

I SEE. SO THAT'S WHAT ODIN'S SIDE HAS BEEN PLANNING. ♡

I WANTED TO SEE FOR MYSELF WHAT KIND OF HUMAN ODIN-CHAN SET HIS EYES ON...

...AND YOU MIGHT BE WORTH A LITTLE MORE OBSERVATION! ♡

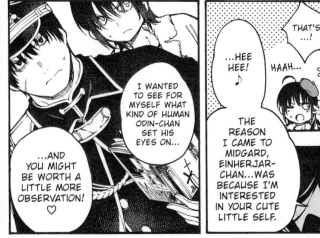

...HEE HEE! ♪

HAAH...

THAT'S...!

ASE (SWEAT)

ASE

ER!

NO!

THE REASON I CAME TO MIDGARD, EINHERJAR-CHAN...WAS BECAUSE I'M INTERESTED IN YOUR CUTE LITTLE SELF.

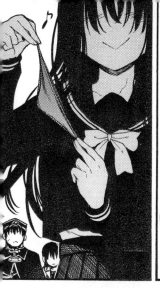

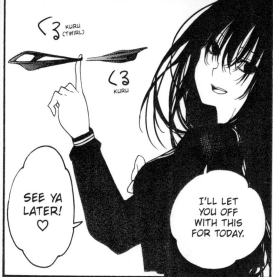

KURU
(TWIRL)

KURU

SEE YA LATER! ♡

I'LL LET YOU OFF WITH THIS FOR TODAY.

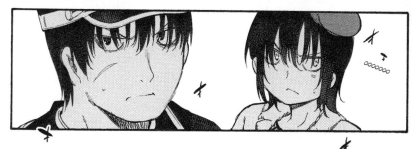

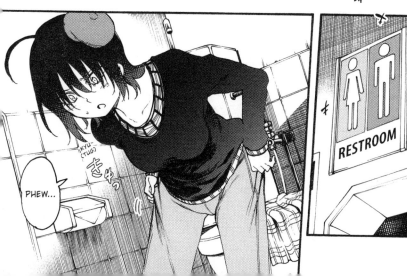

KYU—
(TUG)

PHEW...

RESTROOM

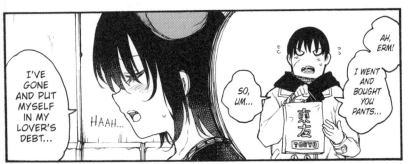

I'VE GONE AND PUT MYSELF IN MY LOVER'S DEBT...

HAAH...

SO, UM...

AH, ERM!

I WENT AND BOUGHT YOU PANTS...

東友 TOBYU

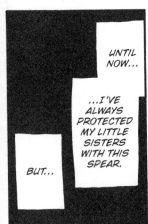

UNTIL NOW...

...I'VE ALWAYS PROTECTED MY LITTLE SISTERS WITH THIS SPEAR.

BUT...

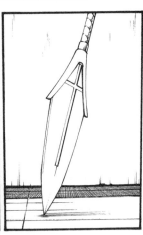

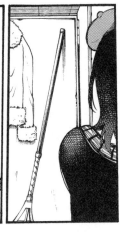

こと、 KOTO (THOK)

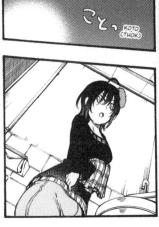

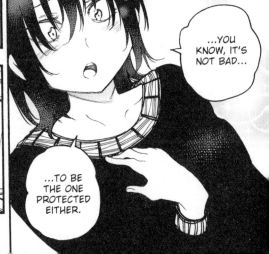

...YOU KNOW, IT'S NOT BAD...

...TO BE THE ONE PROTECTED EITHER.

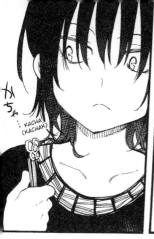
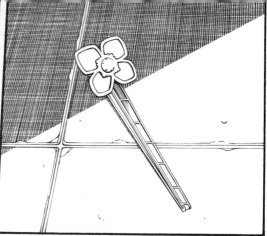

...KACHA!
(KACHAK)

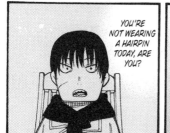

YOU'RE NOT WEARING A HAIRPIN TODAY, ARE YOU?

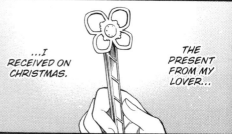

...I RECEIVED ON CHRISTMAS.

THE PRESENT FROM MY LOVER...

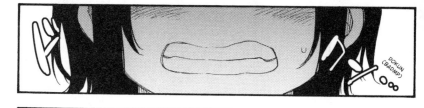

DOKUN
(BADMP)

...AS IF I COULD DO THAT!

AFTER ALL...

...IF I WENT TO THE TROUBLE TO WEAR THIS ON A DATE...

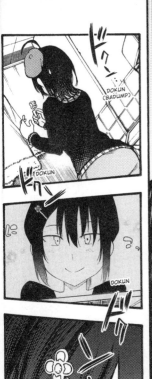

DOKUN
(BADUMP)

DOKUN

DOKUN

DOKUN

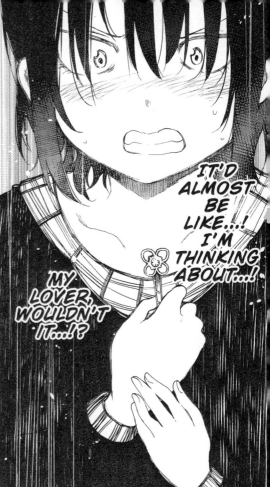

IT'D ALMOST BE LIKE...! I'M THINKING ABOUT...!

MY LOVER, WOULDN'T IT...!?

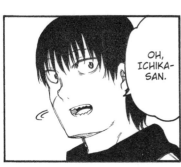

OH, ICHIKA-SAN.

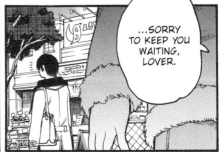

...SORRY TO KEEP YOU WAITING, LOVER.

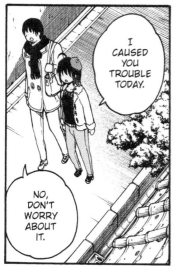

I CAUSED YOU TROUBLE TODAY.

NO, DON'T WORRY ABOUT IT.

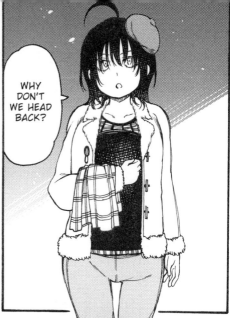

WHY DON'T WE HEAD BACK?

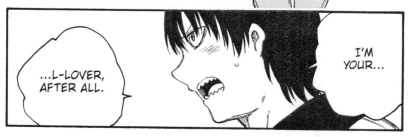

...L-LOVER, AFTER ALL.

I'M YOUR...

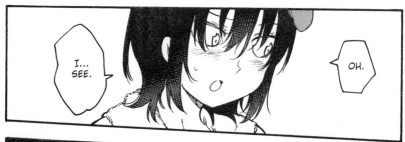

I... SEE.

OH.

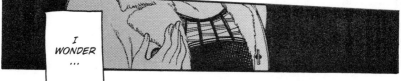

I WONDER...

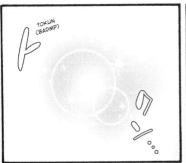

TOKUN (BADMP)

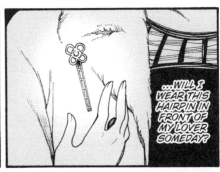

...WILL I WEAR THIS HAIRPIN IN FRONT OF MY LOVER SOMEDAY?

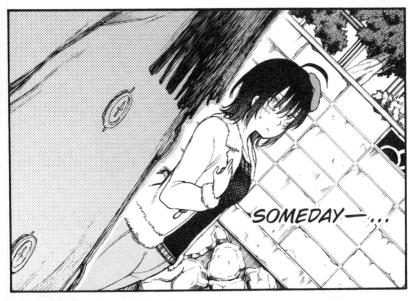

SOMEDAY—...

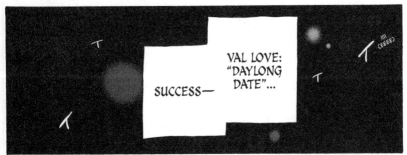

SUCCESS—

VAL LOVE: "DAYLONG DATE"...

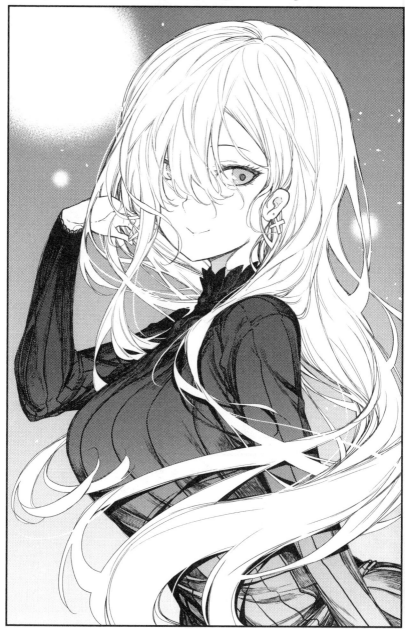

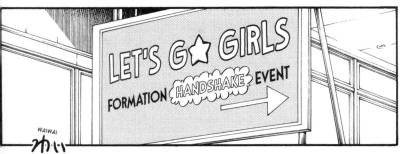

LET'S G☆ GIRLS
FORMATION HANDSHAKE EVENT →

WAIWAI
わいわい

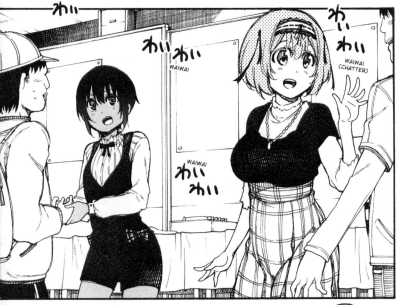

WAIWAI
わい わい

WAIWAI

WAIWAI
(CHATTER)
わい わい

WAIWAI
わい
わい

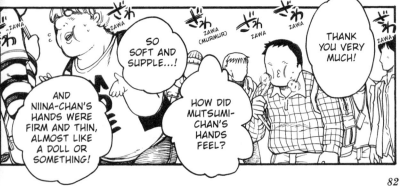

SO SOFT AND SUPPLE...!

AND NIINA-CHAN'S HANDS WERE FIRM AND THIN, ALMOST LIKE A DOLL OR SOMETHING!

HOW DID MUTSUMI-CHAN'S HANDS FEEL?

THANK YOU VERY MUCH!

ZAWA
ZAWA
ZAWA (MURMUR)
ZAWA
ZAWA
ZAWA

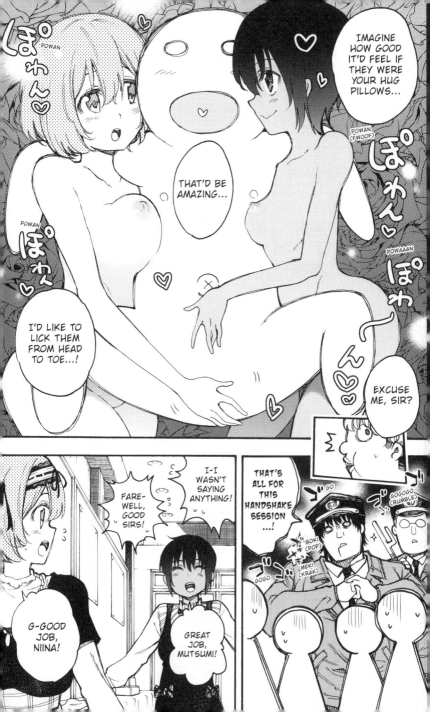

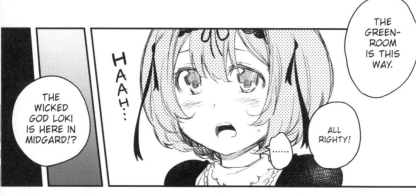

THE GREEN-ROOM IS THIS WAY.

HAAH...

THE WICKED GOD LOKI IS HERE IN MIDGARD!?

......

ALL RIGHTY!

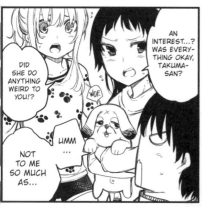

DID SHE DO ANYTHING WEIRD TO YOU!?

AN INTEREST...? WAS EVERY-THING OKAY, TAKUMA-SAN?

WOF

UMM...

NOT TO ME SO MUCH AS...

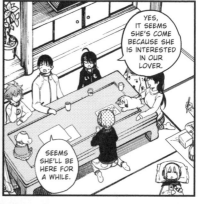

YES, IT SEEMS SHE'S COME BECAUSE SHE IS INTERESTED IN OUR LOVER.

SEEMS SHE'LL BE HERE FOR A WHILE.

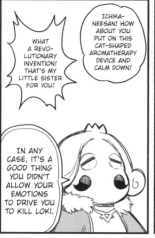

WHAT A REVO-LUTIONARY INVENTION! THAT'S MY LITTLE SISTER FOR YOU!

ICHIKA-NEESAN! HOW ABOUT YOU PUT ON THIS CAT-SHAPED AROMATHERAPY DEVICE AND CALM DOWN!

IN ANY CASE, IT'S A GOOD THING YOU DIDN'T ALLOW YOUR EMOTIONS TO DRIVE YOU TO KILL LOKI.

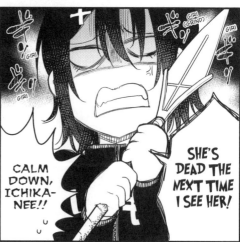

GIRI

GIRI (GRIND)

GIRI

GIRI

GIRI

CALM DOWN, ICHIKA-NEE!!

SHE'S DEAD THE NEXT TIME I SEE HER!

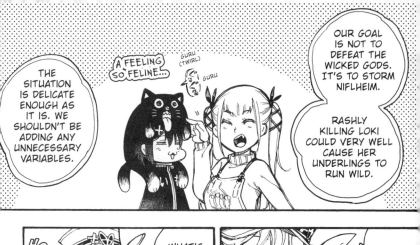

OUR GOAL IS NOT TO DEFEAT THE WICKED GODS. IT'S TO STORM NIFLHEIM.

RASHLY KILLING LOKI COULD VERY WELL CAUSE HER UNDERLINGS TO RUN WILD.

A FEELING SO FELINE...

GURU (TWIRL)

GURU

THE SITUATION IS DELICATE ENOUGH AS IT IS. WE SHOULDN'T BE ADDING ANY UNNECESSARY VARIABLES.

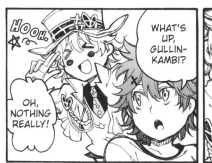

HOOH.

WHAT'S UP, GULLIN-KAMBI?

OH, NOTHING REALLY!

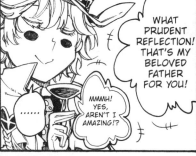

WHAT PRUDENT REFLECTION! THAT'S MY BELOVED FATHER FOR YOU!

......

MMMH! YES, AREN'T I AMAZING!?

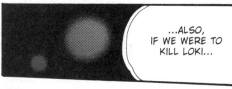

?

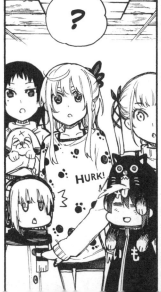

HURK!

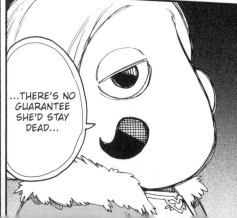

...ALSO, IF WE WERE TO KILL LOKI...

...THERE'S NO GUARANTEE SHE'D STAY DEAD...

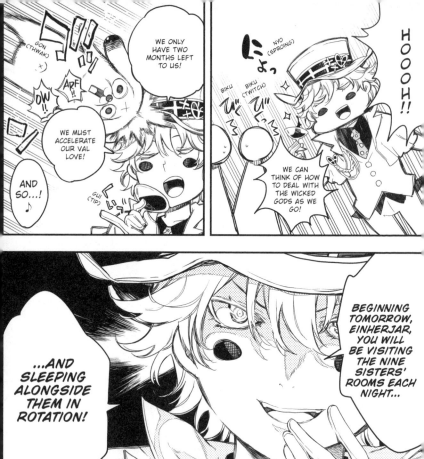

GON (THWAK)

OW!!

ARF!!

WE ONLY HAVE TWO MONTHS LEFT TO US!

WE MUST ACCELERATE OUR VAL LOVE!

AND SO...!

GUI (TIP)

NYO (SPROING)

BIKU (TWITCH)

BIKU (TWITCH)

HOOOH!!

WE CAN THINK OF HOW TO DEAL WITH THE WICKED GODS AS WE GO!

BEGINNING TOMORROW, EINHERJAR, YOU WILL BE VISITING THE NINE SISTERS' ROOMS EACH NIGHT...

...AND SLEEPING ALONGSIDE THEM IN ROTATION!

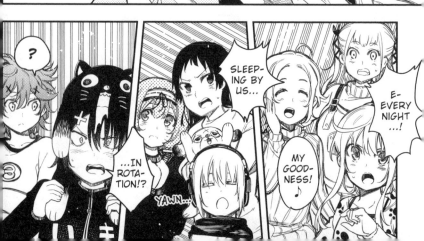

?

...IN ROTATION!?

YAWN...

SLEEP-ING BY US...

MY GOOD-NESS!

E-EVERY NIGHT...!

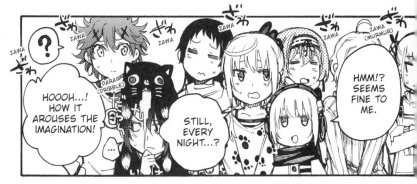

HOOOH...! HOW IT AROUSES THE IMAGINATION!

STILL, EVERY NIGHT...?

HMM!? SEEMS FINE TO ME.

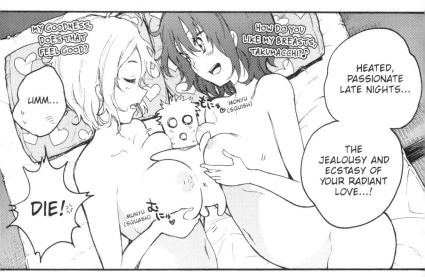

MY GOODNESS, DOES THAT FEEL GOOD?

UMM...

HOW DO YOU LIKE MY BREASTS, TAKUMACCHI?♪

HEATED, PASSIONATE LATE NIGHTS...

THE JEALOUSY AND ECSTASY OF YOUR RADIANT LOVE...!

DIE!

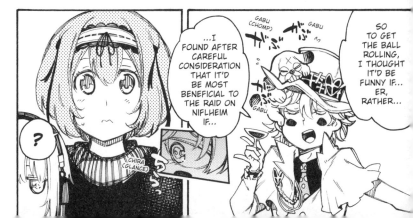

...I FOUND AFTER CAREFUL CONSIDERATION THAT IT'D BE MOST BENEFICIAL TO THE RAID ON NIFLHEIM IF...

SO TO GET THE BALL ROLLING, I THOUGHT IT'D BE FUNNY IF... ER, RATHER...

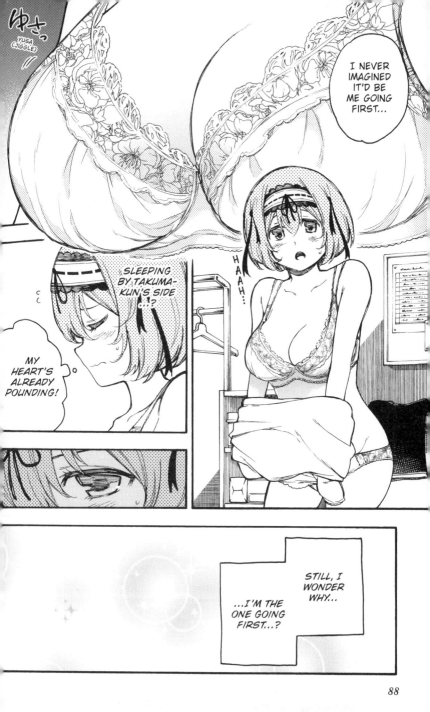

YUSA (JIGGLE)

I NEVER IMAGINED IT'D BE ME GOING FIRST...

SLEEPING BY TAKUMA-KUN'S SIDE ...?

HAAH...

MY HEART'S ALREADY POUNDING!

STILL, I WONDER WHY...

...I'M THE ONE GOING FIRST...?

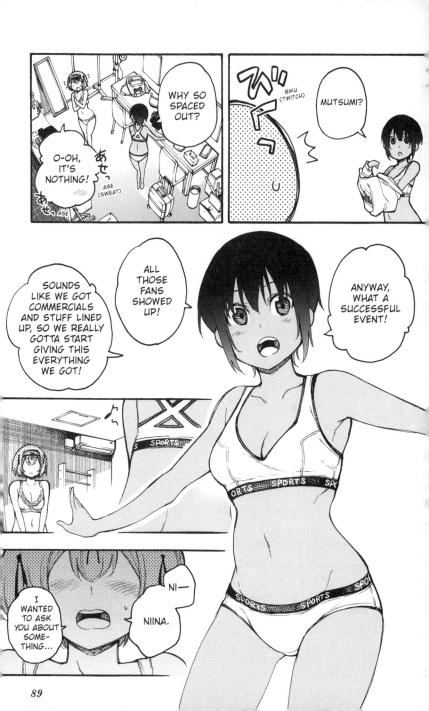

WHY SO SPACED OUT?

O-OH, IT'S NOTHING!

あせっ ASE (SWEAT)

あせ ASE

ビク (TWITCH)

MUTSUMI?

SOUNDS LIKE WE GOT COMMERCIALS AND STUFF LINED UP, SO WE REALLY GOTTA START GIVING THIS EVERYTHING WE GOT!

ALL THOSE FANS SHOWED UP!

ANYWAY, WHAT A SUCCESSFUL EVENT!

SPORTS

I WANTED TO ASK YOU ABOUT SOMETHING...

NI—

NIINA.

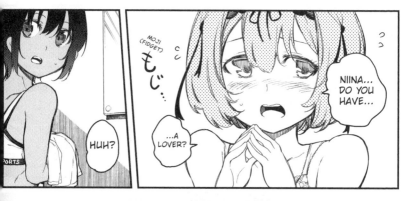

HUH?

MOJI (FIDGET)
もじ…

NIINA... DO YOU HAVE...

...A LOVER?

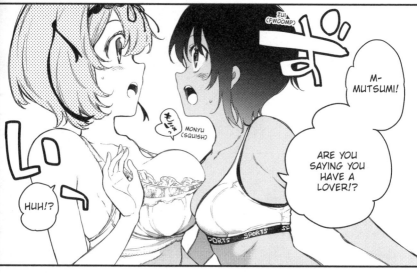

ZUI (FWOOMP)

M-MUTSUMI!

MONYU (SQUISH)

ARE YOU SAYING YOU HAVE A LOVER!?

HUH!?

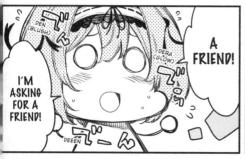

DEN (BLUSH)

DERA (GLOW)

A FRIEND!

I'M ASKING FOR A FRIEND!

DEEEN

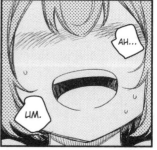

AH...

UM.

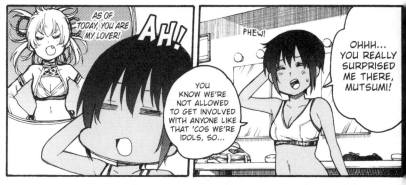

AS OF TODAY, YOU ARE MY LOVER!

AH!

PHEW!

OHHH... YOU REALLY SURPRISED ME THERE, MUTSUMI!

YOU KNOW WE'RE NOT ALLOWED TO GET INVOLVED WITH ANYONE LIKE THAT 'COS WE'RE IDOLS, SO...

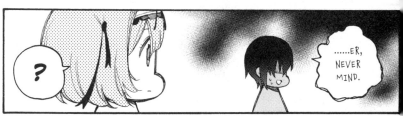

?

......ER, NEVER MIND.

AHEM...

SHE HAS A LOVER.

SO...THIS FRIEND... YOU SEE...?

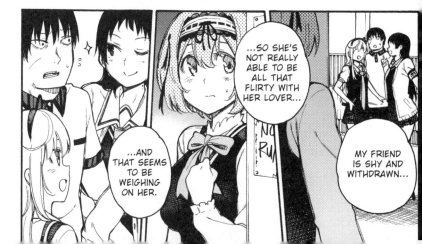

...SO SHE'S NOT REALLY ABLE TO BE ALL THAT FLIRTY WITH HER LOVER...

...AND THAT SEEMS TO BE WEIGHING ON HER.

MY FRIEND IS SHY AND WITHDRAWN...

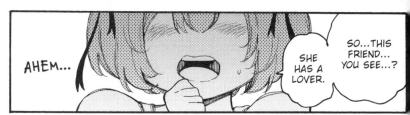

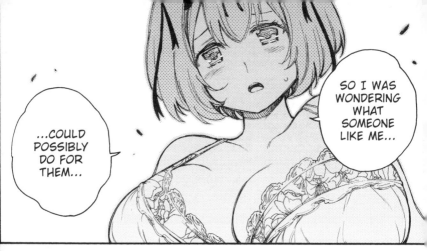

...COULD POSSIBLY DO FOR THEM...

SO I WAS WONDERING WHAT SOMEONE LIKE ME...

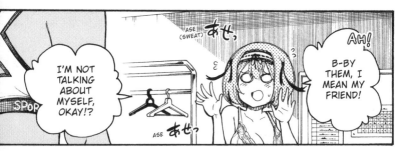

I'M NOT TALKING ABOUT MYSELF, OKAY!?

ASE (SWEAT) あせ、

AH!

B-BY THEM, I MEAN MY FRIEND!

ASE あせっ

SPOR

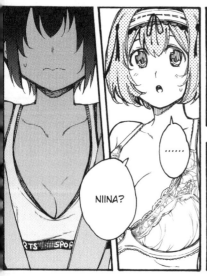

......

NIINA?

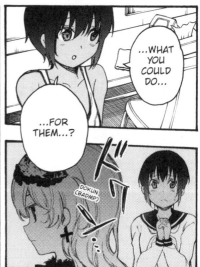

...WHAT YOU COULD DO...

...FOR THEM...?

DOKUN (BADMP)

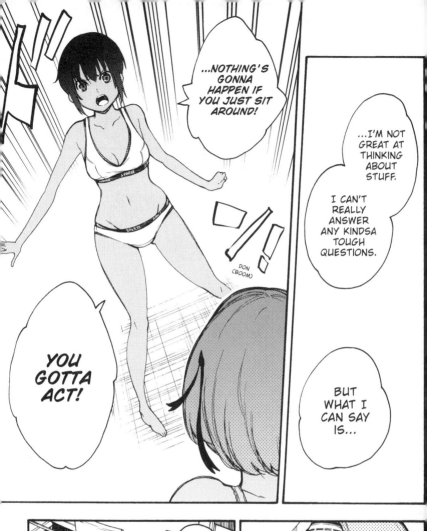

...NOTHING'S GONNA HAPPEN IF YOU JUST SIT AROUND!

...I'M NOT GREAT AT THINKING ABOUT STUFF.

I CAN'T REALLY ANSWER ANY KINDSA TOUGH QUESTIONS.

DON (BOOM)

YOU GOTTA ACT!

BUT WHAT I CAN SAY IS...

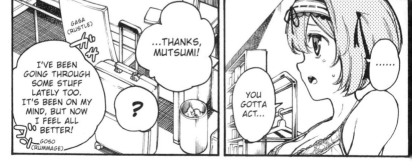

GASA (RUSTLE)

...THANKS, MUTSUMI!

I'VE BEEN GOING THROUGH SOME STUFF LATELY TOO. IT'S BEEN ON MY MIND, BUT NOW I FEEL ALL BETTER!

?

GOSO (RUMMAGE)

......

YOU GOTTA ACT...

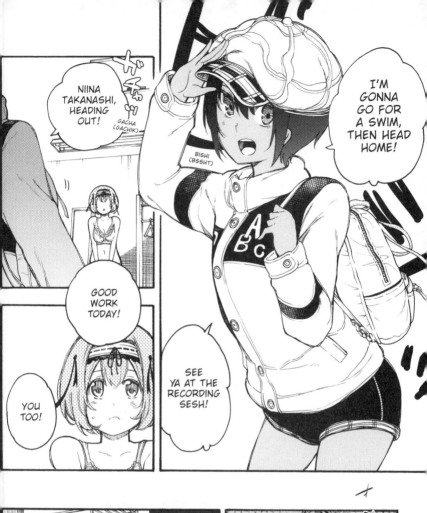

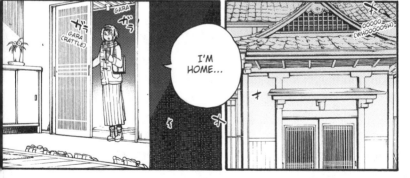

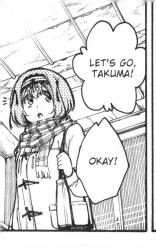

LET'S GO, TAKUMA!

OKAY!

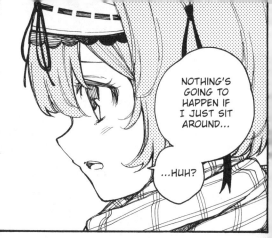

NOTHING'S GOING TO HAPPEN IF I JUST SIT AROUND...

...HUH?

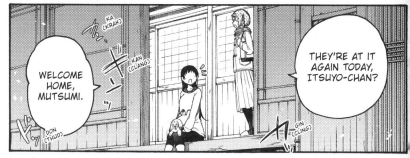

KA (KRAK)

KAN (CLANG)

WELCOME HOME, MUTSUMI.

THEY'RE AT IT AGAIN TODAY, ITSUYO-CHAN?

DON (THUD)

GIN (CLING)

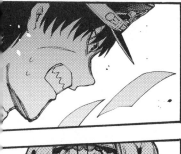

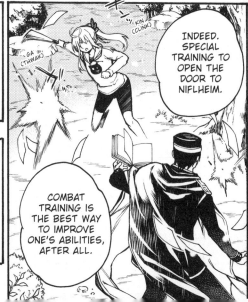

KIN (CLINK)

INDEED. SPECIAL TRAINING TO OPEN THE DOOR TO NIFLHEIM.

GA (THWAK)

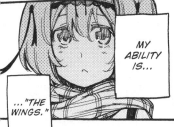

MY ABILITY IS...

..."THE WINGS."

COMBAT TRAINING IS THE BEST WAY TO IMPROVE ONE'S ABILITIES, AFTER ALL.

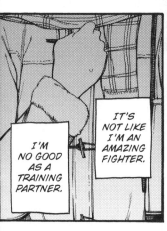

I'M NO GOOD AS A TRAINING PARTNER.

IT'S NOT LIKE I'M AN AMAZING FIGHTER.

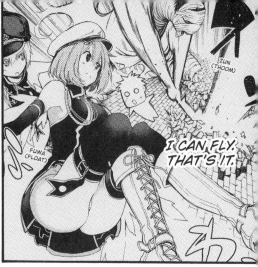

FUWA (FLOAT)

ZUN (THOOM)

I CAN FLY. THAT'S IT.

...THEY ARE SO LUCKY.

THEY CAN HELP TAKUMA-KUN GROW STRONGER.

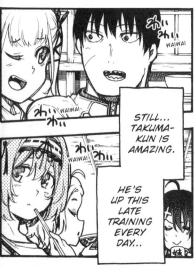

WAIWAI

WAIWAI

STILL... TAKUMA-KUN IS AMAZING.

HE'S UP THIS LATE TRAINING EVERY DAY...

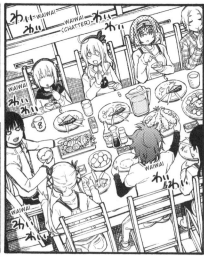

WAIWAI

WAIWAI (CHATTER)

WAIWAI

WAIWAI

WAIWAI

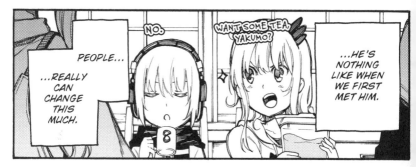

PEOPLE...

...REALLY CAN CHANGE THIS MUCH.

NO.

WANT SOME TEA, YAKUMO?

...HE'S NOTHING LIKE WHEN WE FIRST MET HIM.

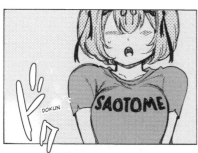

SAOTOME

DOKUN

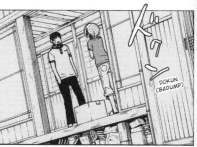

DOKUN (BADUMP)

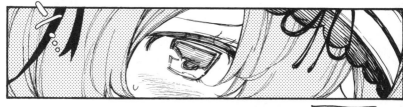

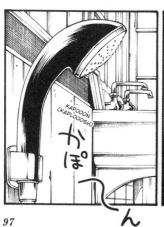

KAPOOON (KAPLOOOSH)

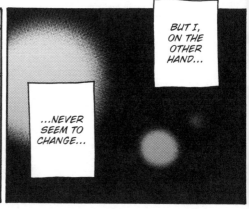

BUT I, ON THE OTHER HAND...

...NEVER SEEM TO CHANGE...

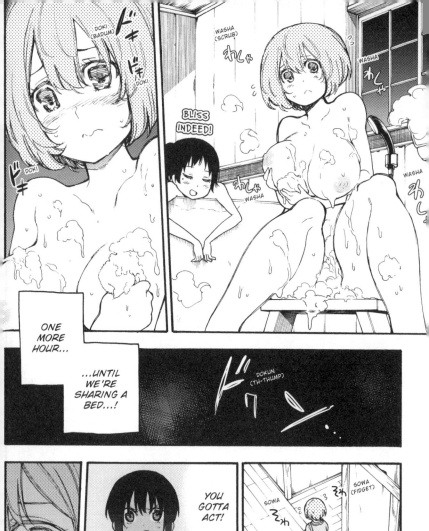

ONE MORE HOUR...

...UNTIL WE'RE SHARING A BED...!

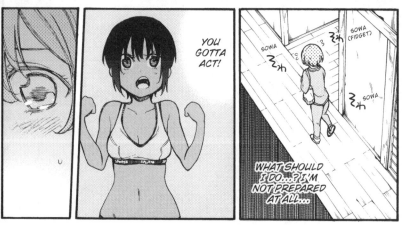

YOU GOTTA ACT!

WHAT SHOULD I DO...? I'M NOT PREPARED AT ALL...

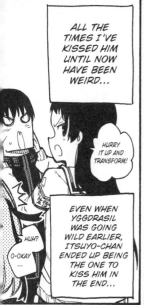

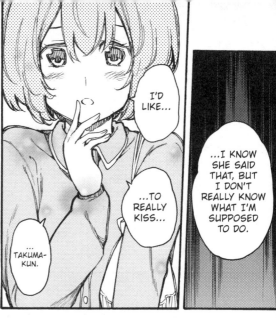

ALL THE TIMES I'VE KISSED HIM UNTIL NOW HAVE BEEN WEIRD...

HURRY IT UP AND TRANSFORM!

EVEN WHEN YGGDRASIL WAS GOING WILD EARLIER, ITSUYO-CHAN ENDED UP BEING THE ONE TO KISS HIM IN THE END...

HUH?

O-OKAY...

I'D LIKE...

...TO REALLY KISS...

...TAKUMA-KUN.

...I KNOW SHE SAID THAT, BUT I DON'T REALLY KNOW WHAT I'M SUPPOSED TO DO.

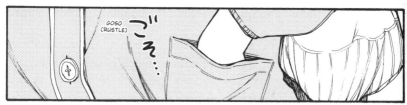

GOSO (RUSTLE)

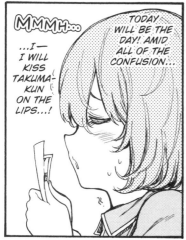

MMMH...

...I—I WILL KISS TAKUMA-KUN ON THE LIPS...!

TODAY WILL BE THE DAY! AMID ALL OF THE CONFUSION...

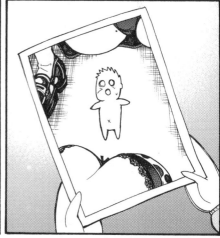

PARA
(CRUMBLE)

SLEIPNIR-SAMA
WAS CHASING
ME, SO...
ARE YOUR
PREPARATIONS
FOR THIS
FINE NIGHT
PROCEEDING
WELL?

G-GOOD
EVENING,
GULLINKAMBI-
SAN...!

WHY'D YOU
COME FROM THE
WALL...?

UH.

BAKYA
(BA-KRAKK)

HYEEK!?

GOOD
DAY TO YOU,
HELMWIGE-
SAMA!

GUSHA
(SCRUNCH)

AH...

Y-YES...

UM...

SOWA
(FIDGET)

SOWA

SOWA

MOJI
(SQUIRM)
も
じ

I'M...

...WERE
YOU AWARE,
HELMWIGE-
SAMA?

...FINE.

I
THINK
...

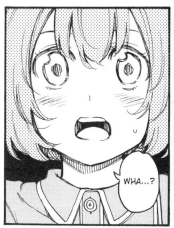

WHA...?

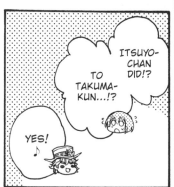

ITSUYO-CHAN DID!?

TO TAKUMA-KUN...!?

YES!

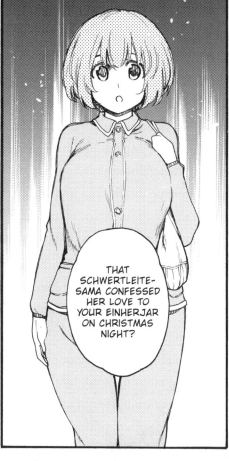

THAT SCHWERTLEITE-SAMA CONFESSED HER LOVE TO YOUR EINHERJAR ON CHRISTMAS NIGHT?

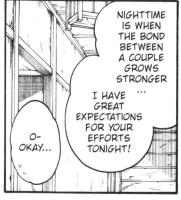

NIGHTTIME IS WHEN THE BOND BETWEEN A COUPLE GROWS STRONGER

I HAVE GREAT EXPECTATIONS FOR YOUR EFFORTS TONIGHT!

O-OKAY...

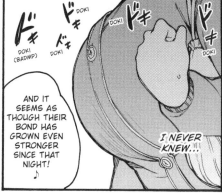

DOKI

DOKI (BADMP)

DOKI

DOKI

DOKI

DOKI

AND IT SEEMS AS THOUGH THEIR BOND HAS GROWN EVEN STRONGER SINCE THAT NIGHT!

I NEVER KNEW...

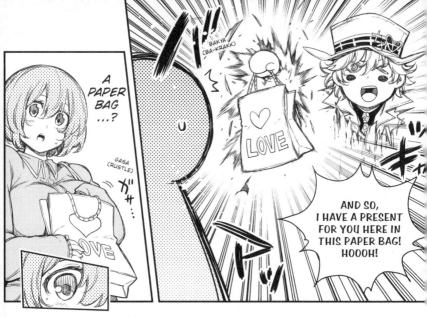

A PAPER BAG ...?

GASA (RUSTLE)

BAKYA (BA-KRAKK)

LOVE

AND SO, I HAVE A PRESENT FOR YOU HERE IN THIS PAPER BAG! HOOOH!

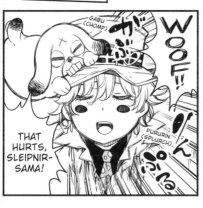

WOOF!!

GABU (CHOMP)

THAT HURTS, SLEIPNIR-SAMA!

PURURIN (SPLURCH)

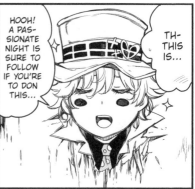

HOOH! A PASSIONATE NIGHT IS SURE TO FOLLOW IF YOU'RE TO DON THIS...

TH-THIS IS...

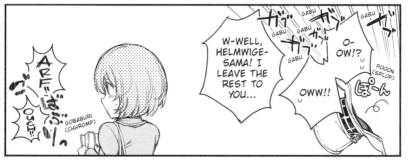

W-WELL, HELMWIGE-SAMA! I LEAVE THE REST TO YOU...

ARF!!

OUCH!!

GOBABURI (CHHROMP)

GABU GABU GABU GABU

O-OW!?

OWW!!

POOON (SPLOP)

102

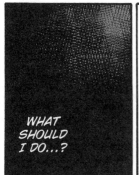

WHAT SHOULD I DO...?

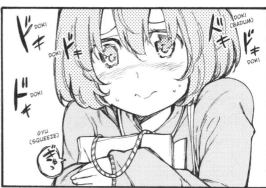

DOKI!

DOKI!

DOKI (BADUM)

DOKI!

DOKI

GYU (SQUEEZE)

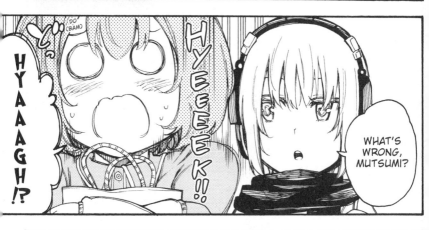

DO! (BAM)

HYAAAGH!?

HYEEEK!!

WHAT'S WRONG, MUTSUMI?

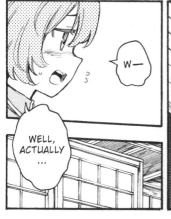

W—

WELL, ACTUALLY...

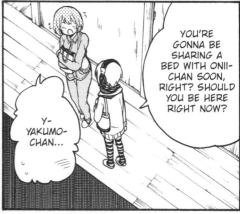

YOU'RE GONNA BE SHARING A BED WITH ONII-CHAN SOON, RIGHT? SHOULD YOU BE HERE RIGHT NOW?

Y-YAKUMO-CHAN...

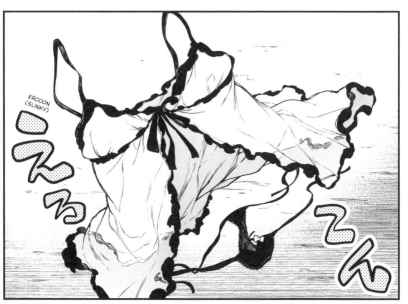

EROOON
(SLINKY)

GULLIN-KAMBI-SAN GAVE IT TO ME, AND...

HUH. REAL NAUGHTY.

SEE-THROUGH!

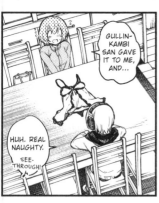

WH∘∘∘ ∘∘∘OA—

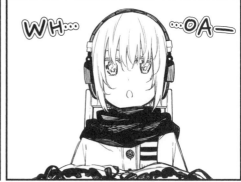

BIKUUUN
(JOLT)

FWUH!?

ONII-CHAN WILL LOVE IT IF YOU WEAR THIS.

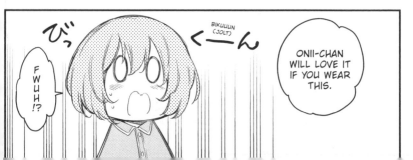

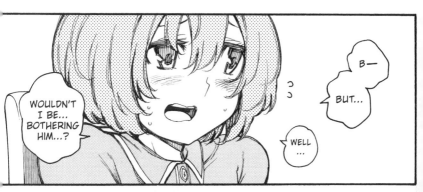

WOULDN'T I BE... BOTHERING HIM...?

B— BUT...

WELL...

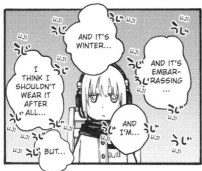

I THINK I SHOULDN'T WEAR IT AFTER ALL...

AND IT'S WINTER...

AND IT'S EMBARRASSING...

AND I'M...

BUT...

UJI

UJI

UJI

UJI

UJI

UJI

UJI

UJI

UJI

UJI

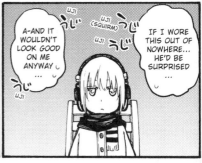

A-AND IT WOULDN'T LOOK GOOD ON ME ANYWAY...

IF I WORE THIS OUT OF NOWHERE... HE'D BE SURPRISED...

UJI

UJI

UJI (SQUIRM)

UJI

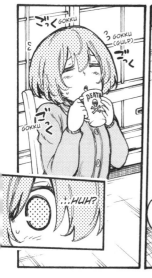

GOKKU

GOKKU (GULP)

GOKKU

DEATH

...HUH?

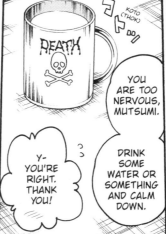

DEATH

KOTO (THOK)

YOU ARE TOO NERVOUS, MUTSUMI.

DRINK SOME WATER OR SOMETHING AND CALM DOWN.

Y-YOU'RE RIGHT. THANK YOU!

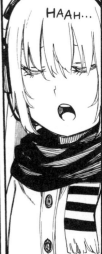

HAAH...

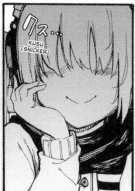

KUSU
(SNICKER)

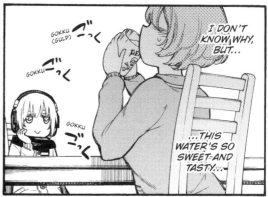

GOKKU
(GULP)

GOKKU

GOKKU

I DON'T KNOW WHY, BUT...

...THIS WATER'S SO SWEET-AND TASTY...

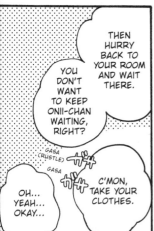

THEN HURRY BACK TO YOUR ROOM AND WAIT THERE.

YOU DON'T WANT TO KEEP ONII-CHAN WAITING, RIGHT?

GASA
(RUSTLE)

GASA

OH... YEAH... OKAY...

C'MON, TAKE YOUR CLOTHES.

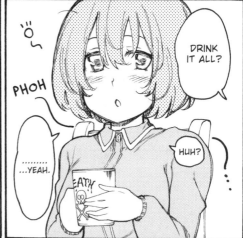

PHOH

DRINK IT ALL?

HUH?

....
...YEAH.

EATH

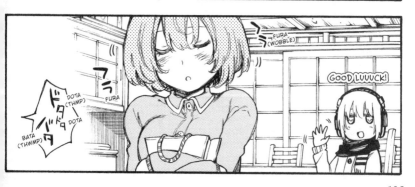

DOTA
(THMP)

DOTA

FURA

BATA
(THWMP)

FURA
(WOBBLE)

GOOD LUUUCK!

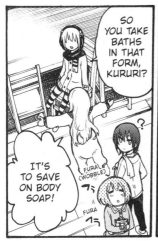

SO YOU TAKE BATHS IN THAT FORM, KURURI?

IT'S TO SAVE ON BODY SOAP!

?

FURA (WOBBLE)

FURA

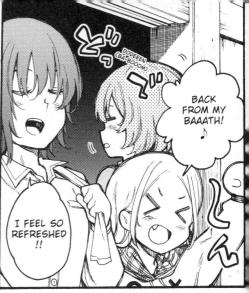

DODEEEN (BA-BOOM)

BACK FROM MY BAAATH!

I FEEL SO REFRESHED!!

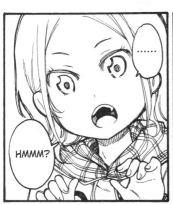

......

HMMM?

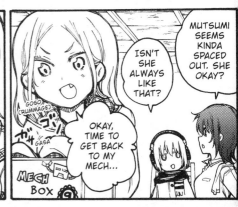

MUTSUMI SEEMS KINDA SPACED OUT. SHE OKAY?

ISN'T SHE ALWAYS LIKE THAT?

OKAY, TIME TO GET BACK TO MY MECH...

GOSO (RUMMAGE)

GASA

MECH BOX

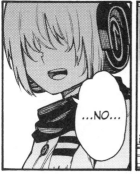

...NO...

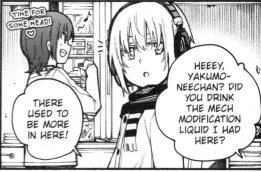

TIME FOR SOME MEAD!

THERE USED TO BE MORE IN HERE!

HEEEY, YAKUMO-NEECHAN? DID YOU DRINK THE MECH MODIFICATION LIQUID I HAD HERE?

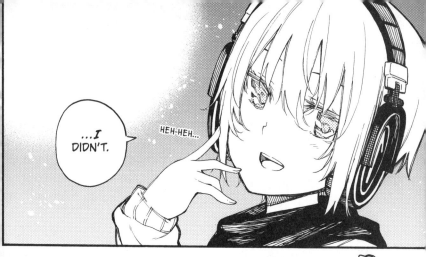

HEH-HEH...

...I DIDN'T.

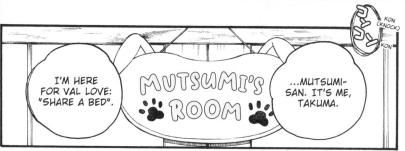

KON (KNOCK)
KON

I'M HERE FOR VAL LOVE: "SHARE A BED".

MUTSUMI'S ROOM

...MUTSUMI-SAN. IT'S ME, TAKUMA.

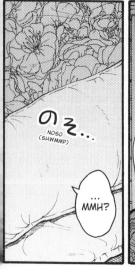

のそ...
NOSO (SHWMMP)

...MMH?

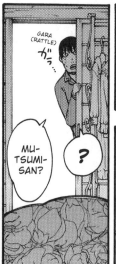

GARA (RATTLE)
が...

MU-TSUMI-SAN?

?

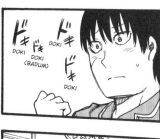

ド゙ギ DOKI
ド゙ギ DOKI (BADUM)
ド゙ギ DOKI
ド゙ギ DOKI!

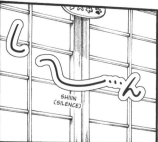

し〜〜ん
SHIIIN (SILENCE)

108

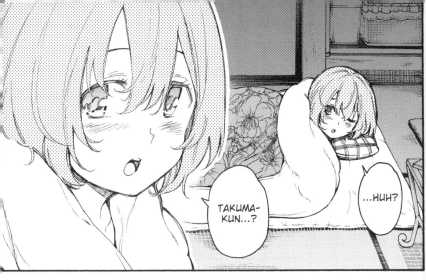

TAKUMA-KUN...?

...HUH?

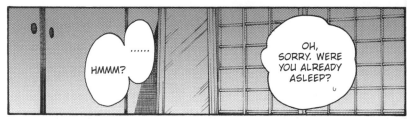

......

HMMM?

OH, SORRY. WERE YOU ALREADY ASLEEP?

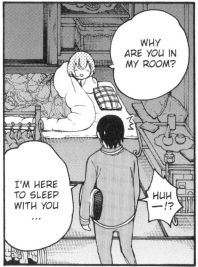

WHY ARE YOU IN MY ROOM?

I'M HERE TO SLEEP WITH YOU ...

HUH —!?

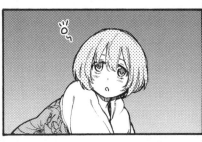

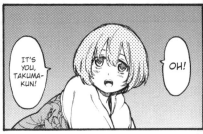

IT'S YOU, TAKUMA-KUN!

OH!

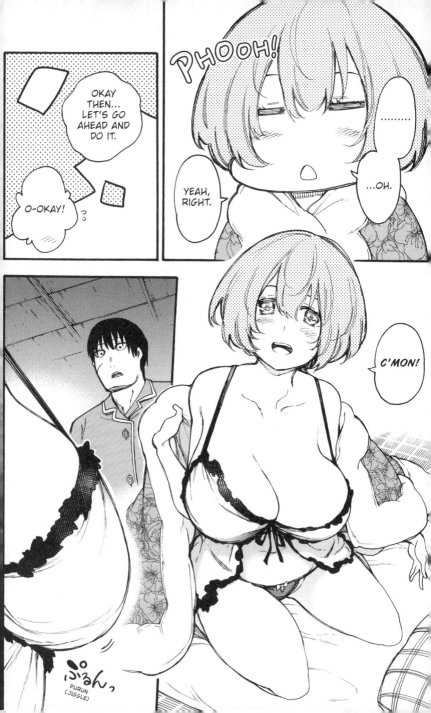

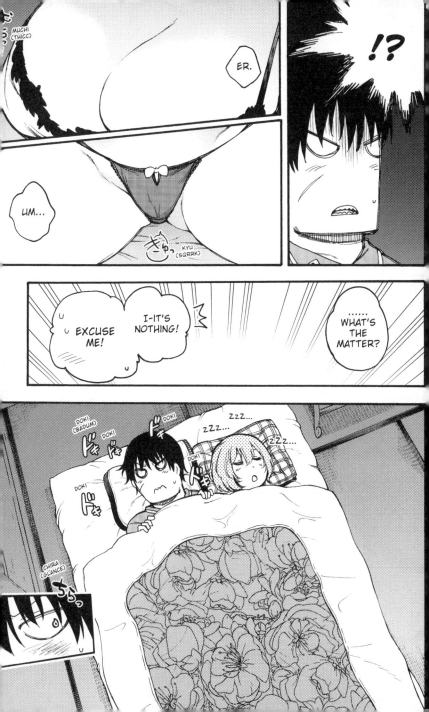

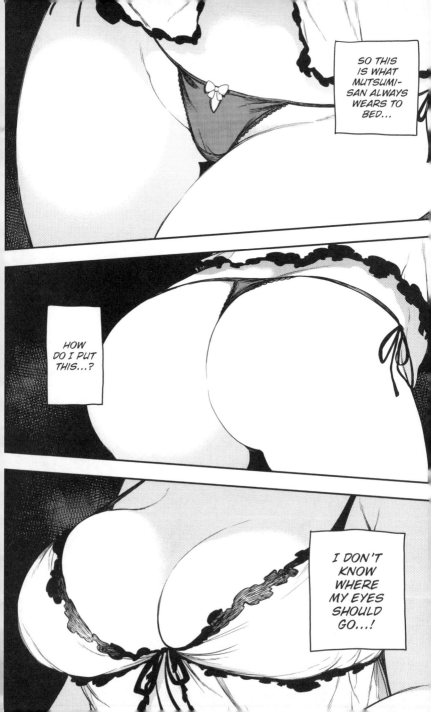

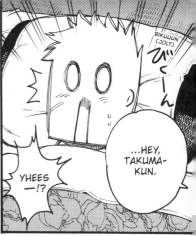

BIKUUUN (JOLT)

...HEY, TAKUMA-KUN.

YHEES —!?

IS IT TRUE THAT ITSUYO-CHAN TOLD YOU SHE HAS FEELINGS FOR YOU?

HUH?

UMM...

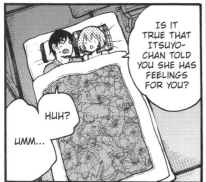

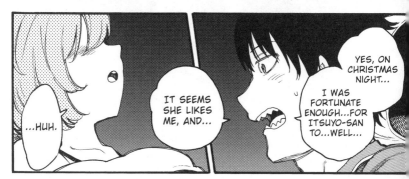

...HUH.

IT SEEMS SHE LIKES ME, AND...

YES, ON CHRISTMAS NIGHT...

I WAS FORTUNATE ENOUGH...FOR ITSUYO-SAN TO...WELL...

?

...HEY, TAKUMA-KUN.

SO IT MADE YOU HAP...

...PY?

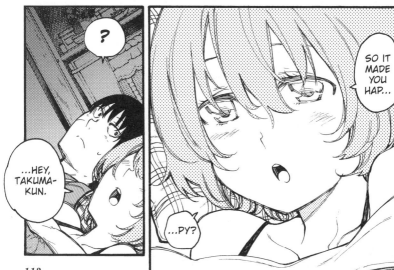

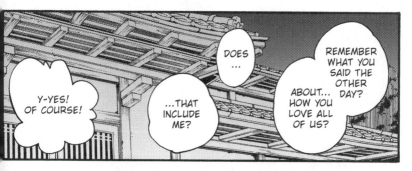

REMEMBER WHAT YOU SAID THE OTHER DAY?

DOES...

...ABOUT... HOW YOU LOVE ALL OF US?

...THAT INCLUDE ME?

Y-YES! OF COURSE!

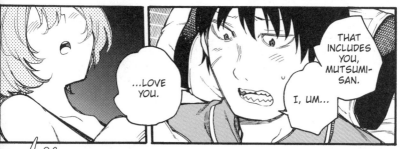

...LOVE YOU.

THAT INCLUDES YOU, MUTSUMI-SAN.

I, UM...

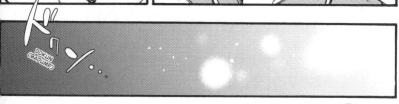

DO-UN
(BADUMP)

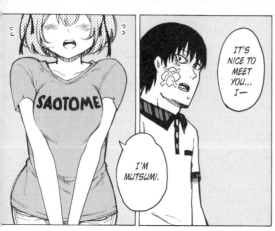

SAOTOME

I'M MUTSUMI.

IT'S NICE TO MEET YOU... I—

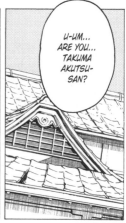

U-UM... ARE YOU... TAKUMA AKUTSU-SAN?

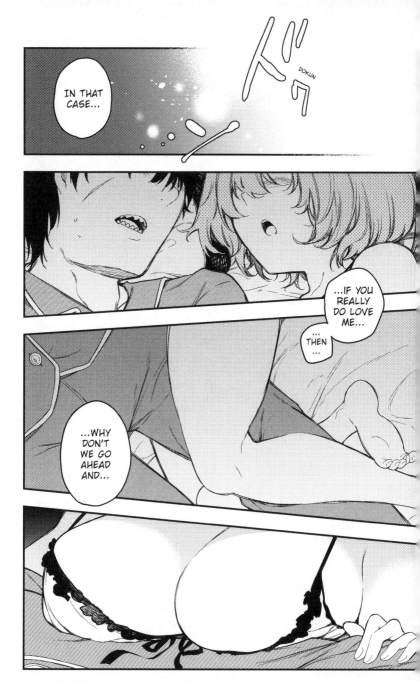

115

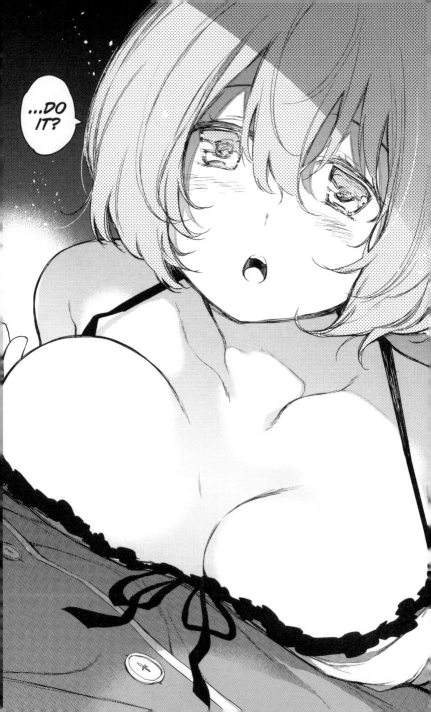

Chapter 58: The Kissing Maiden 2

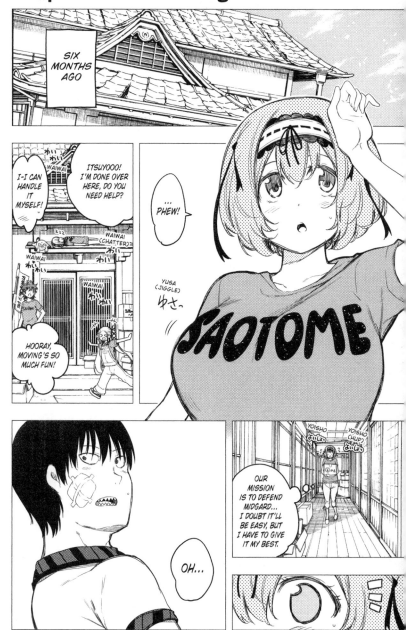

SIX MONTHS AGO

... PHEW!

YUSA (JIGGLE)
ゆさっ

SAOTOME

WAIWAI
かいかい

I-I CAN HANDLE IT MYSELF!

ITSUYOOO! I'M DONE OVER HERE, DO YOU NEED HELP?

WAIWAI (CHATTER)

WAIWAI
かいかい

WAIWAI

HOORAY, MOVING'S SO MUCH FUN!

YOISHO
どっしょ

YOISHO (CHUG)
どっしょ

OUR MISSION IS TO DEFEND MIDGARD... I DOUBT IT'LL BE EASY, BUT I HAVE TO GIVE IT MY BEST.

OH...

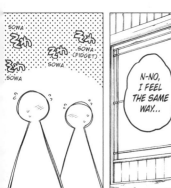

SOWA SOWA (FIDGET) SOWA SOWA

N-NO, I FEEL THE SAME WAY...

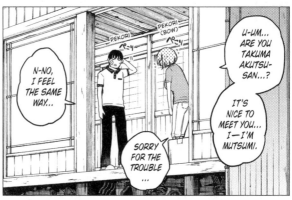

PEKORI PEKORI (BOW)

U-UM... ARE YOU TAKUMA AKUTSU-SAN...?

IT'S NICE TO MEET YOU... I—I'M MUTSUMI.

SORRY FOR THE TROUBLE ...

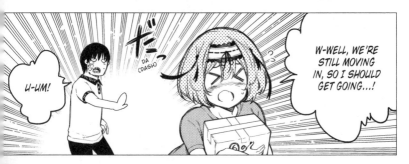

U-UM!

DA (DASH)

W-WELL, WE'RE STILL MOVING IN, SO I SHOULD GET GOING...!

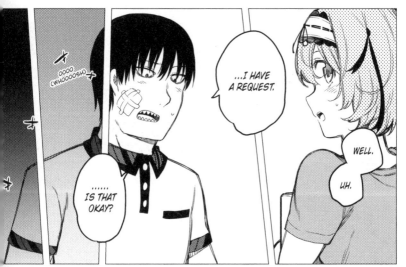

OOOO (WHOOOOSH)

...I HAVE A REQUEST.

WELL.

UH.

...... IS THAT OKAY?

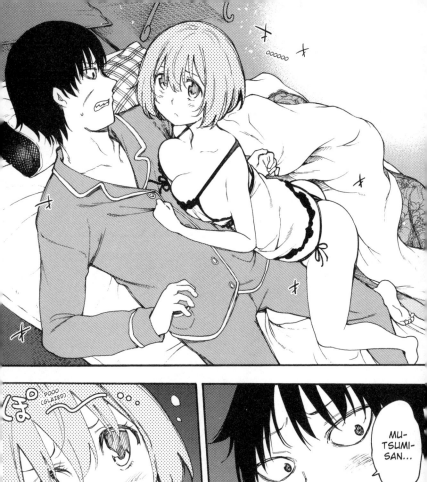

POOO
(GLAZED)

MU-
TSUMI-
SAN...

...I
KNEW
IT.

YOU
DON'T
WANT
TO DO IT
WITH ME.

WHAT
DO YOU
MEAN...

...BY
D-DO
IT?

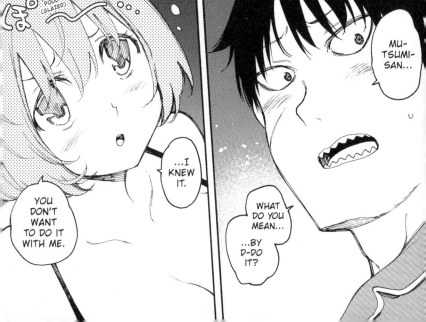

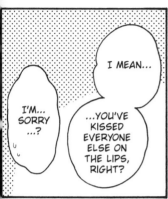

I'M... SORRY ...?

I MEAN...

...YOU'VE KISSED EVERYONE ELSE ON THE LIPS, RIGHT?

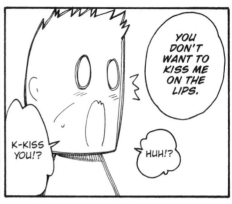

YOU DON'T WANT TO KISS ME ON THE LIPS.

K-KISS YOU!?

HUH!?

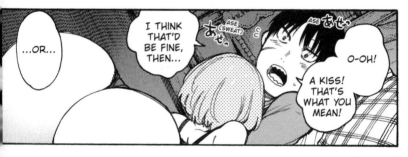

...OR...

I THINK THAT'D BE FINE, THEN...

ASE (SWEAT)

ASE

O-OH!

A KISS! THAT'S WHAT YOU MEAN!

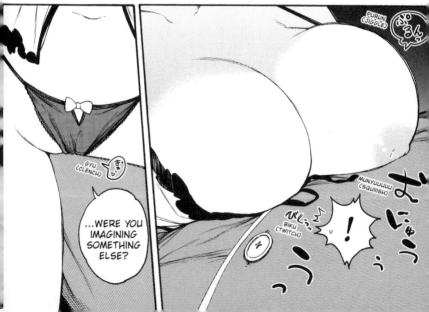

PURUN (JIGGLE)

GYU (CLENCH)

...WERE YOU IMAGINING SOMETHING ELSE?

MUNYUUUUU (SQUIIISH)

BIKU (TWITCH)

!

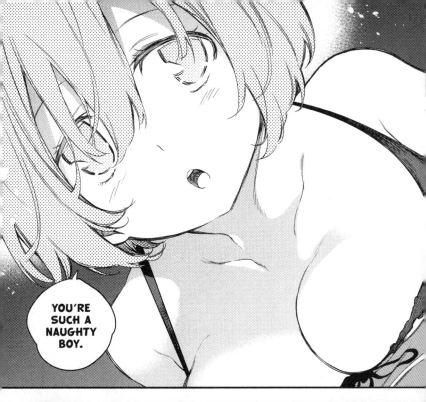

YOU'RE SUCH A NAUGHTY BOY.

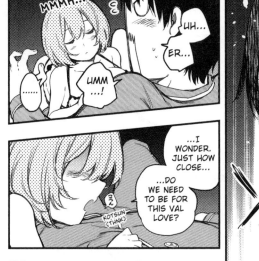

MMMH...

UH...

ER...

......

UMM ...!

...I WONDER. JUST HOW CLOSE...

...DO WE NEED TO BE FOR THIS VAL LOVE?

KOTSUN (THNK)

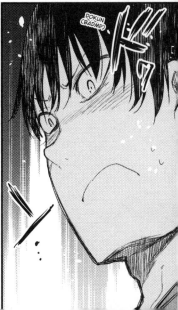

DOKUN (BADMP)

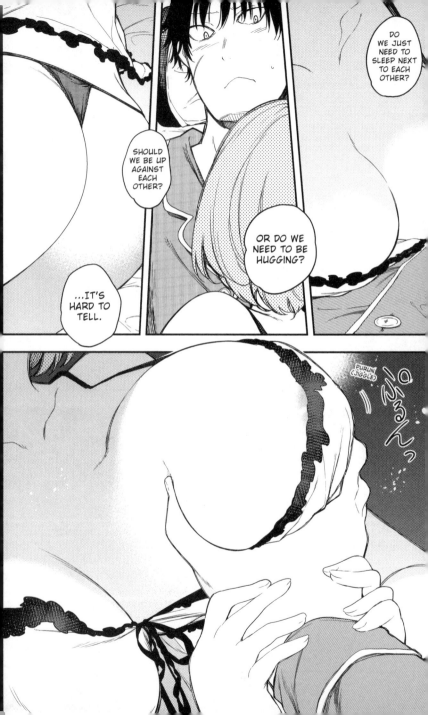

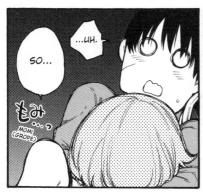

SO...

...UH.

もみ
MOMI
(GROPE)

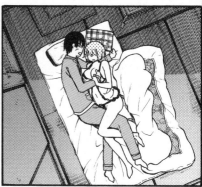

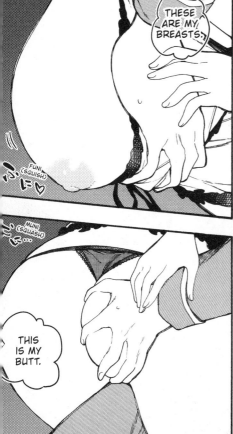

THESE ARE MY BREASTS.

ふに♡
FUNI
(SQUISH)

むに♡
MUNI
(SQUASH)

THIS IS MY BUTT.

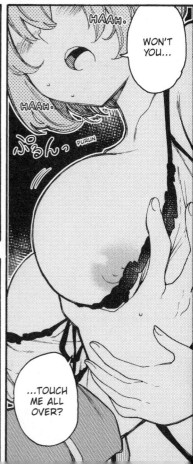

HAAH.

WON'T YOU...

HAAH.

ぷるんっ
PURUN

...TOUCH ME ALL OVER?

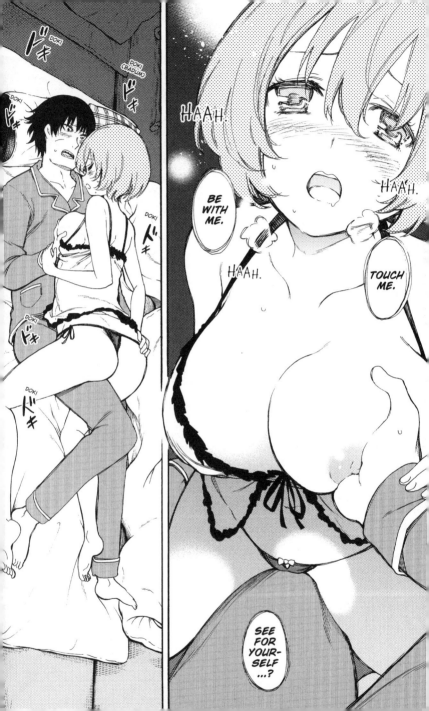

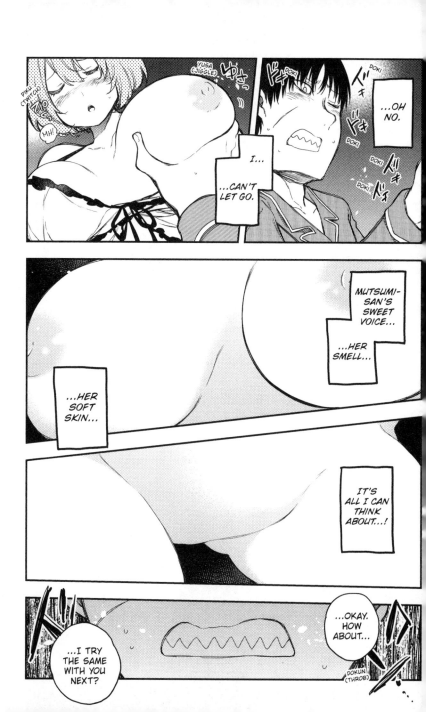

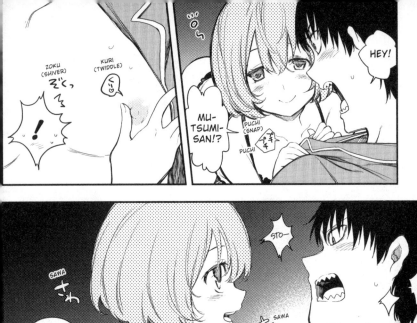

ZOKU
(SHIVER)

KURI
(TWIDDLE)

HEY!

MU-
TSUMI-
SAN!?

PUCHI
(SNAP)

PUCHI

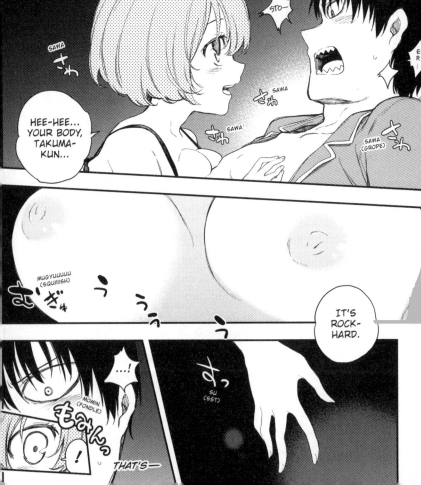

SAWA

STO—

ER
...

SAWA

SAWA

SAWA

SAWA
(GROPE)

HEE-HEE...
YOUR BODY,
TAKUMA-
KUN...

MUGYUUUUU
(SQUIIIISH)

IT'S
ROCK-
HARD.

...!

MOMIN
(FONDLE)

SU
(SST)

THAT'S—

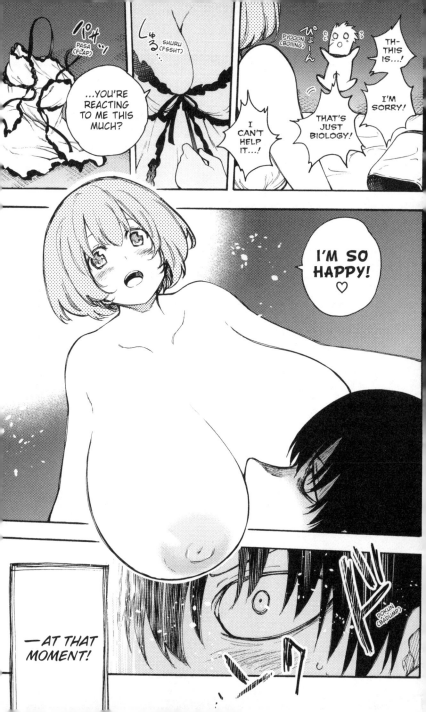

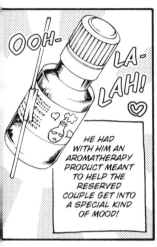

OOH-LA-LAH! ♡

HE HAD WITH HIM AN AROMATHERAPY PRODUCT MEANT TO HELP THE RESERVED COUPLE GET INTO A SPECIAL KIND OF MOOD!

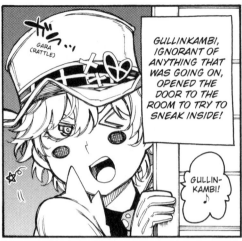

GARA (RATTLE)

GULLINKAMBI, IGNORANT OF ANYTHING THAT WAS GOING ON, OPENED THE DOOR TO THE ROOM TO TRY TO SNEAK INSIDE!

GULLIN-KAMBI! ♪

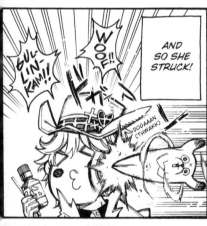

GULLINKAM!!

WOOF!!

DOGAAAN (THWACK)

AND SO SHE STRUCK!

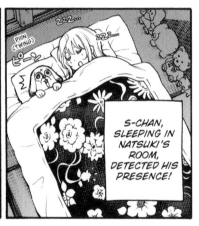

ZZZ...

PIIN (TWING)

ピーン

ZZZ...

S-CHAN, SLEEPING IN NATSUKI'S ROOM, DETECTED HIS PRESENCE!

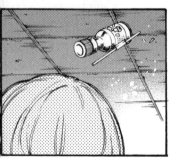

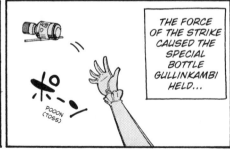

POOON (TOSS)

THE FORCE OF THE STRIKE CAUSED THE SPECIAL BOTTLE GULLINKAMBI HELD...

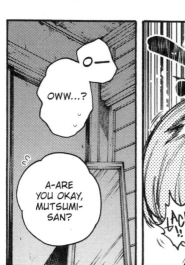

OWW...?

A-ARE YOU OKAY, MUTSUMI-SAN?

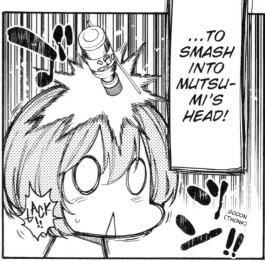

...TO SMASH INTO MUTSU-MI'S HEAD!

GOOON (THONK)

TACK!!

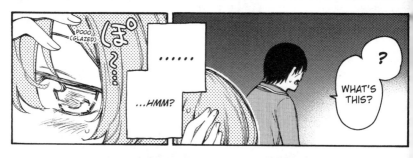

POOO (GLAZED)

......

...HMM?

?

WHAT'S THIS?

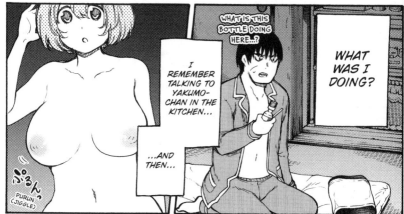

WHAT IS THIS BOTTLE DOING HERE...?

I REMEMBER TALKING TO YAKUMO-CHAN IN THE KITCHEN...

...AND THEN...

WHAT WAS I DOING?

PURUN, (JIGGLE)

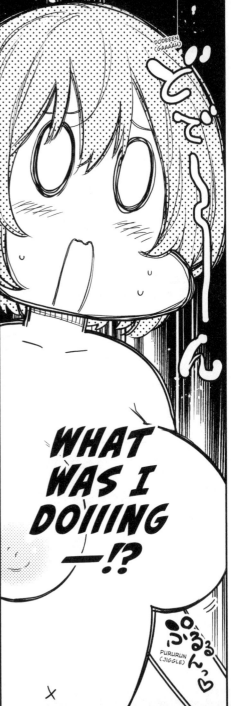

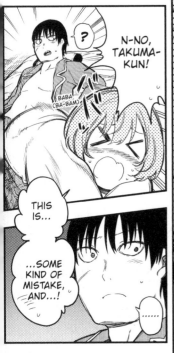

N-NO, TAKUMA-KUN!

BABA (BA-BAM)

THIS IS...

...SOME KIND OF MISTAKE, AND...!

......

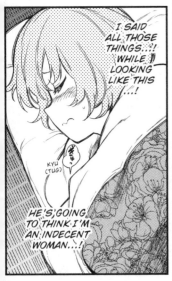

I SAID ALL THOSE THINGS...! WHILE LOOKING LIKE THIS...!

KYU (TUG)

HE'S GOING TO THINK I'M AN INDECENT WOMAN...!

DODEEEN (GAAAAH)

WHAT WAS I DOIIING —!?

PURURUN (JIGGLE)

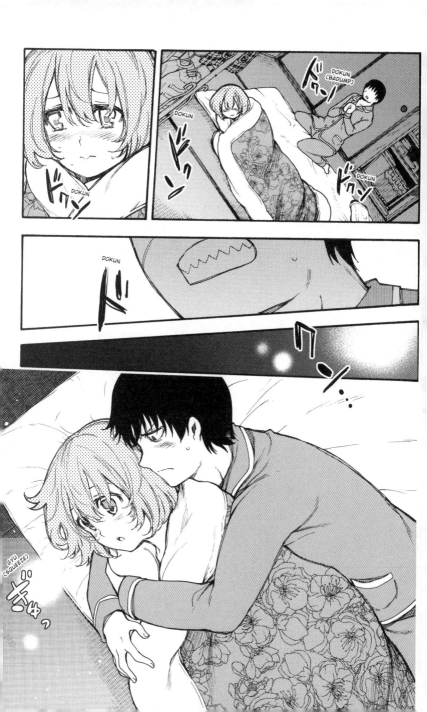

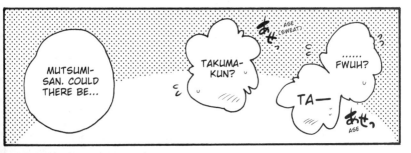

MUTSUMI-SAN. COULD THERE BE...

TAKUMA-KUN?

あせっ (SWEAT)

....
FWUH?

TA—

あせっ ASE

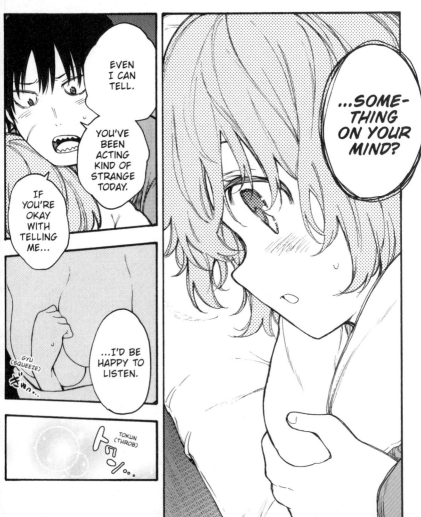

EVEN I CAN TELL.

YOU'VE BEEN ACTING KIND OF STRANGE TODAY.

IF YOU'RE OKAY WITH TELLING ME...

...I'D BE HAPPY TO LISTEN.

GYU (SQUEEZE)

ぎゅぅ...

...SOME-THING ON YOUR MIND?

TOKUN (THROB)

トゥ...

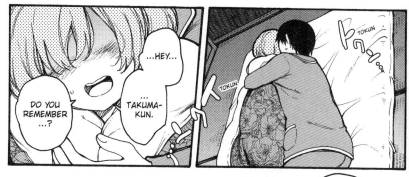

...HEY...

DO YOU REMEMBER...?

...TAKUMA-KUN.

TOKUN

TOKUN

TOKUN

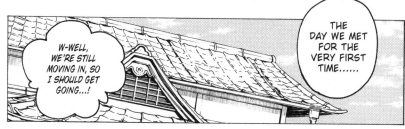

W-WELL, WE'RE STILL MOVING IN, SO I SHOULD GET GOING...!

THE DAY WE MET FOR THE VERY FIRST TIME......

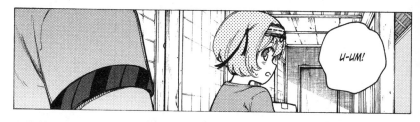

U-UM!

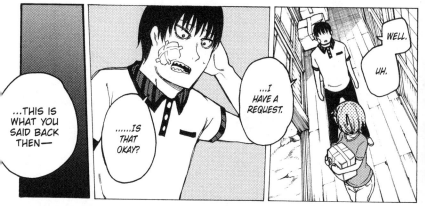

...THIS IS WHAT YOU SAID BACK THEN—

......IS THAT OKAY?

...I HAVE A REQUEST.

WELL, UH.

133

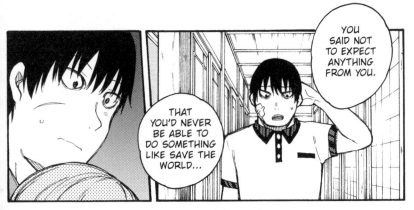

YOU SAID NOT TO EXPECT ANYTHING FROM YOU.

THAT YOU'D NEVER BE ABLE TO DO SOMETHING LIKE SAVE THE WORLD...

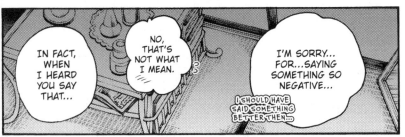

IN FACT, WHEN I HEARD YOU SAY THAT...

NO, THAT'S NOT WHAT I MEAN.

I'M SORRY... FOR...SAYING SOMETHING SO NEGATIVE...

I SHOULD HAVE SAID SOMETHING BETTER THEN...

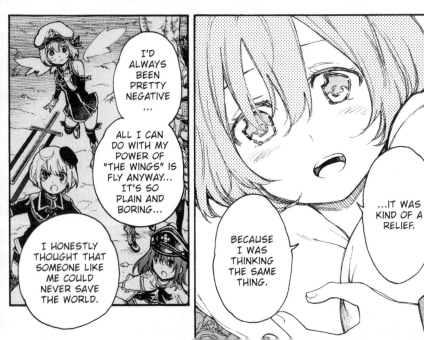

I'D ALWAYS BEEN PRETTY NEGATIVE...

ALL I CAN DO WITH MY POWER OF "THE WINGS" IS FLY ANYWAY... IT'S SO PLAIN AND BORING...

I HONESTLY THOUGHT THAT SOMEONE LIKE ME COULD NEVER SAVE THE WORLD.

BECAUSE I WAS THINKING THE SAME THING.

...IT WAS KIND OF A RELIEF.

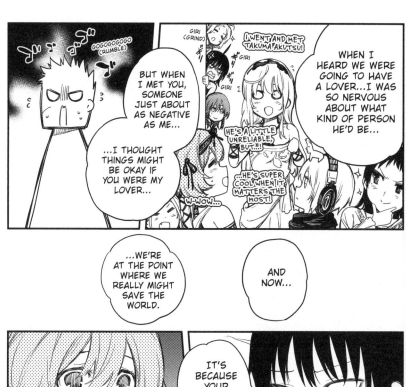

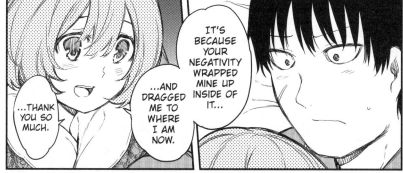

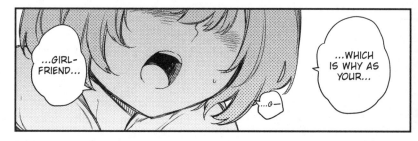

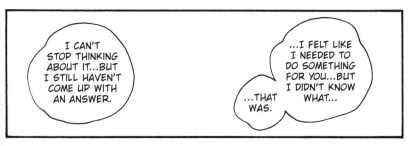

I CAN'T STOP THINKING ABOUT IT...BUT I STILL HAVEN'T COME UP WITH AN ANSWER.

...I FELT LIKE I NEEDED TO DO SOMETHING FOR YOU...BUT I DIDN'T KNOW WHAT...

...THAT WAS.

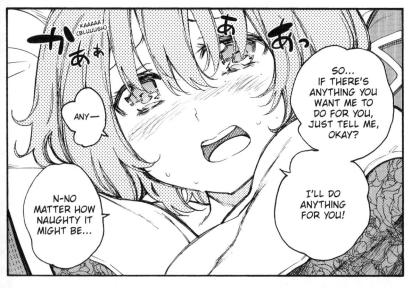

KAAAAA (BLUUUSH)

ANY—

SO... IF THERE'S ANYTHING YOU WANT ME TO DO FOR YOU, JUST TELL ME, OKAY?

N-NO MATTER HOW NAUGHTY IT MIGHT BE...

I'LL DO ANYTHING FOR YOU!

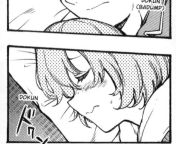

DOKUN (BADUMP)

DOKUN

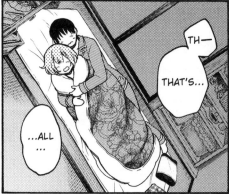

TH—

THAT'S...

...ALL ...

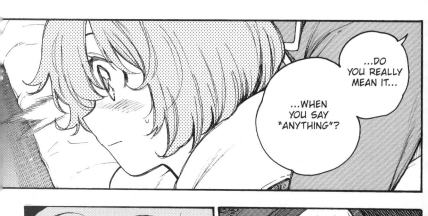

...DO YOU REALLY MEAN IT...

...WHEN YOU SAY "ANYTHING"?

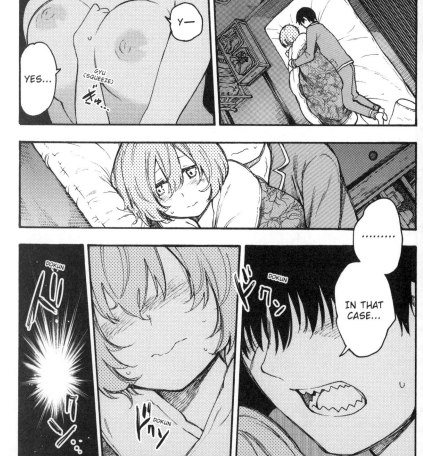

Y—

YES...

GYU (SQUEEZE)

....

IN THAT CASE...

DOKUN

DOKUN

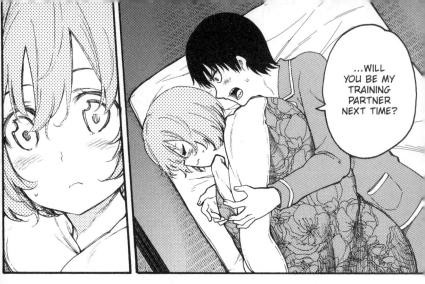

...WILL YOU BE MY TRAINING PARTNER NEXT TIME?

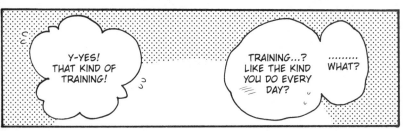

Y-YES! THAT KIND OF TRAINING!

TRAINING...? LIKE THE KIND YOU DO EVERY DAY?

....
WHAT?

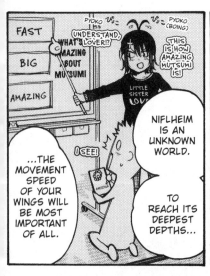

FAST

BIG

AMAZING

PYOKO (UNDERSTAND, WHAT'S LOVER!? AMAZING ABOUT MUTSUMI!)

PYOKO (BOING)

THIS IS HOW AMAZING MUTSUMI IS!

LITTLE SISTER LOVE

I SEE!

NIFLHEIM IS AN UNKNOWN WORLD.

...THE MOVEMENT SPEED OF YOUR WINGS WILL BE MOST IMPORTANT OF ALL.

TO REACH ITS DEEPEST DEPTHS...

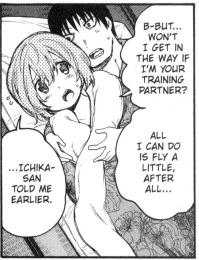

B-BUT... WON'T I GET IN THE WAY IF I'M YOUR TRAINING PARTNER?

ALL I CAN DO IS FLY A LITTLE, AFTER ALL...

...ICHIKA-SAN TOLD ME EARLIER.

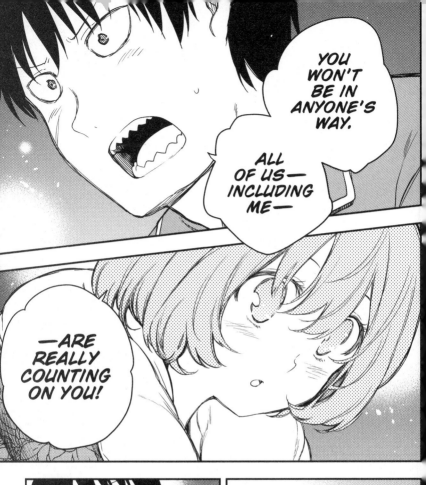

YOU WON'T BE IN ANYONE'S WAY.

ALL OF US— INCLUDING ME—

—ARE REALLY COUNTING ON YOU!

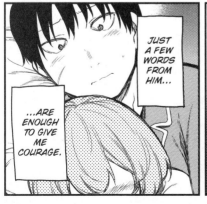

JUST A FEW WORDS FROM HIM...

...ARE ENOUGH TO GIVE ME COURAGE.

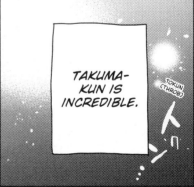

TAKUMA-KUN IS INCREDIBLE.

(TOKUN) (THROB)

トクン

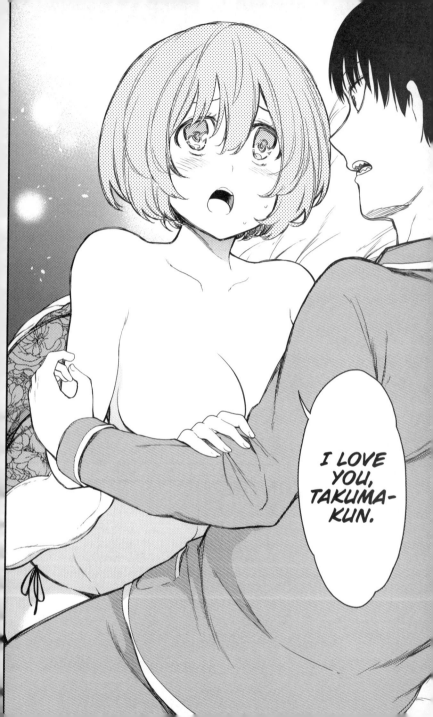

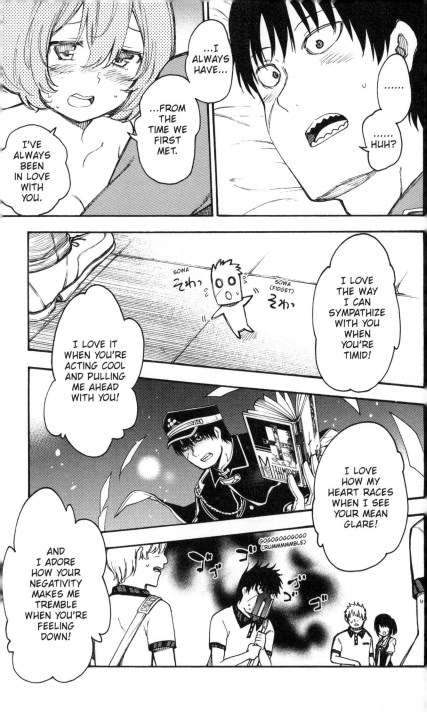

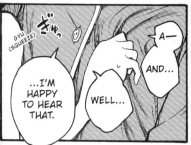

GYU
(SQUEEZE)

A—

AND...

...I'M HAPPY TO HEAR THAT.

WELL...

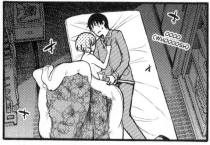

OOOO
(WHOOOOSH)

...THANK YOU.

HEARING YOU SAY THAT YOU LOVE ME, MUTSUMI-SAN...

...MAKES ME REALLY HAPPY.

TOKUN
(BADMP)

I KNOW...

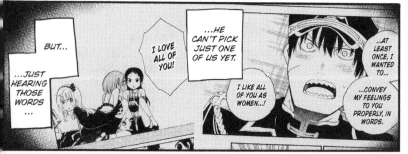

BUT...

...JUST HEARING THOSE WORDS...

I LOVE ALL OF YOU!

...HE CAN'T PICK JUST ONE OF US YET.

I LIKE ALL OF YOU AS WOMEN...!

...AT LEAST ONCE, I WANTED TO...

...CONVEY MY FEELINGS TO YOU PROPERLY, IN WORDS.

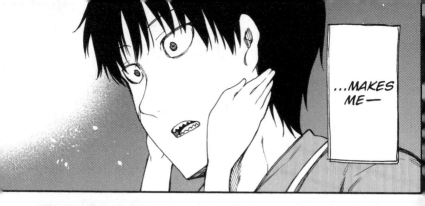

...MAKES ME—

MUTSUMI-SA—

DOKI (THROB)

...?

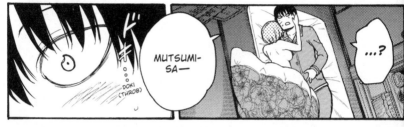

DOKUN (BADUMP)

DOKUN

DOKUN

DOKUN

DOKUN

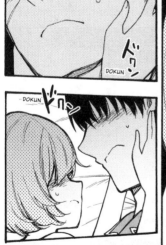

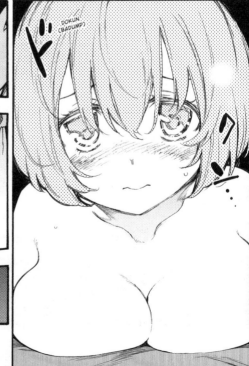

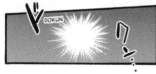

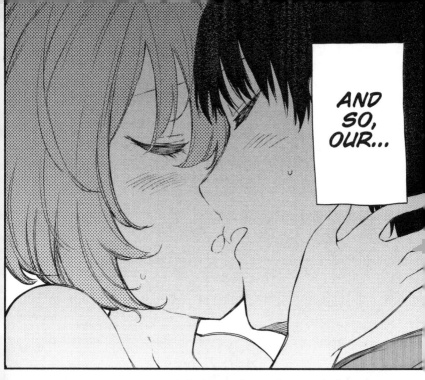

AND SO, OUR...

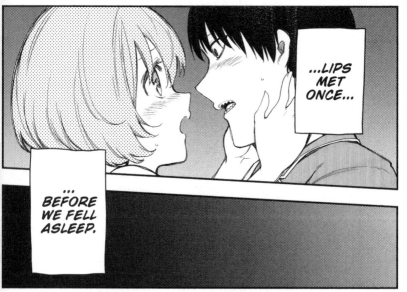

...LIPS MET ONCE...

...BEFORE WE FELL ASLEEP.

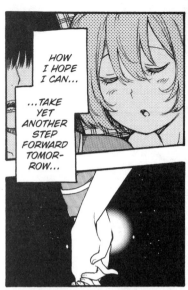

HOW I HOPE I CAN...

...TAKE YET ANOTHER STEP FORWARD TOMOR-ROW...

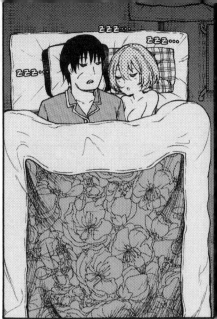

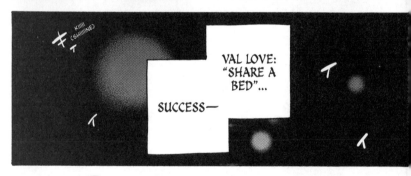

VAL LOVE: "SHARE A BED"...

SUCCESS—

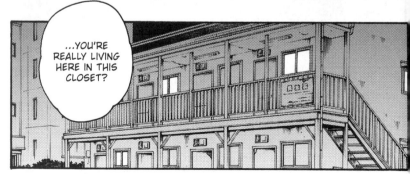

...YOU'RE REALLY LIVING HERE IN THIS CLOSET?

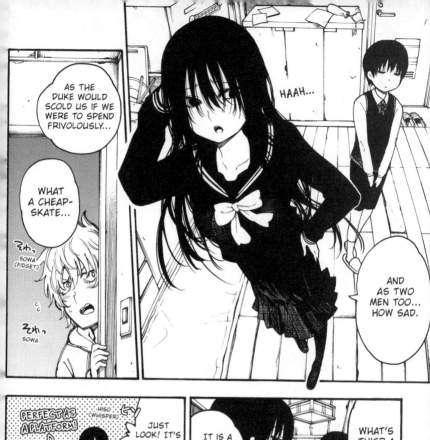

AS THE DUKE WOULD SCOLD US IF WE WERE TO SPEND FRIVOLOUSLY...

WHAT A CHEAP-SKATE...

ぞわ
SOWA (FIDGET)

ぞわ
SOWA

HAAH...

AND AS TWO MEN TOO... HOW SAD.

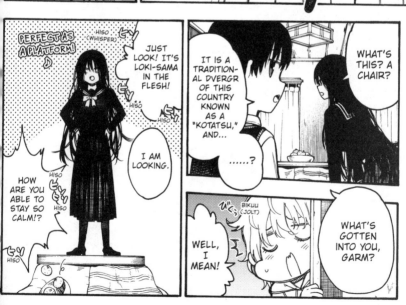

PERFECT AS A PLATFORM!

HISO (WHISPER)

JUST LOOK! IT'S LOKI-SAMA IN THE FLESH!

HISO

HISO

I AM LOOKING.

HOW ARE YOU ABLE TO STAY SO CALM!?

HISO

HISO

HISO

IT IS A TRADITIONAL DVERGR OF THIS COUNTRY KNOWN AS A "KOTATSU," AND...

......?

WHAT'S THIS? A CHAIR?

び"く
BIKUU (JOLT)

WELL, I MEAN!

WHAT'S GOTTEN INTO YOU, GARM?

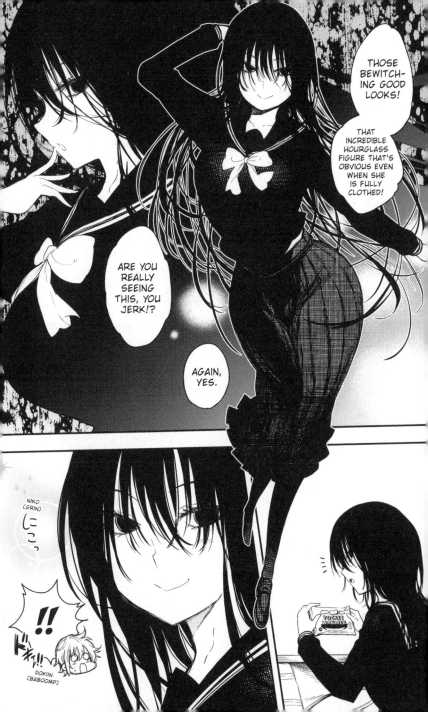

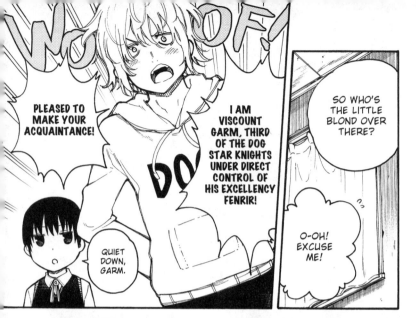

PLEASED TO MAKE YOUR ACQUAINTANCE!

I AM VISCOUNT GARM, THIRD OF THE DOG STAR KNIGHTS UNDER DIRECT CONTROL OF HIS EXCELLENCY FENRIR!

QUIET DOWN, GARM.

SO WHO'S THE LITTLE BLOND OVER THERE?

O-OH! EXCUSE ME!

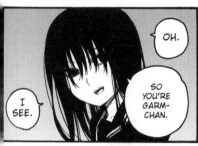

OH.

I SEE.

SO YOU'RE GARM-CHAN.

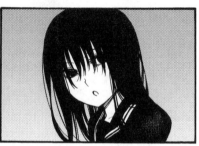

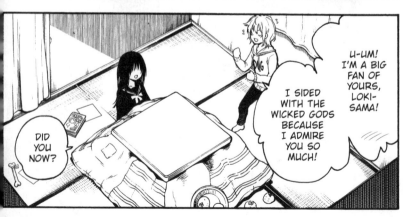

DID YOU NOW?

I SIDED WITH THE WICKED GODS BECAUSE I ADMIRE YOU SO MUCH!

U-UM! I'M A BIG FAN OF YOURS, LOKI-SAMA!

148

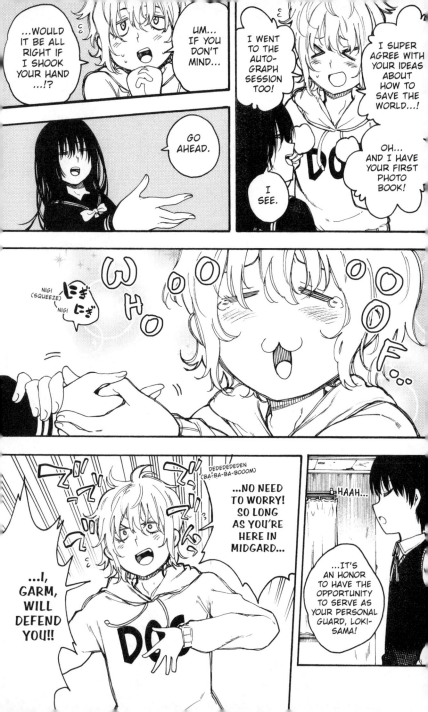

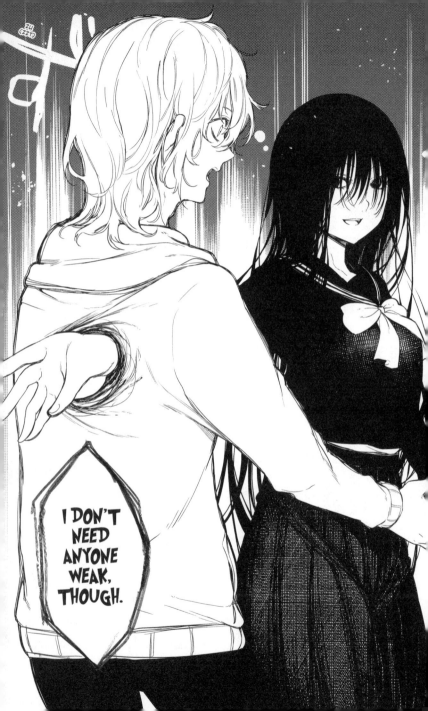

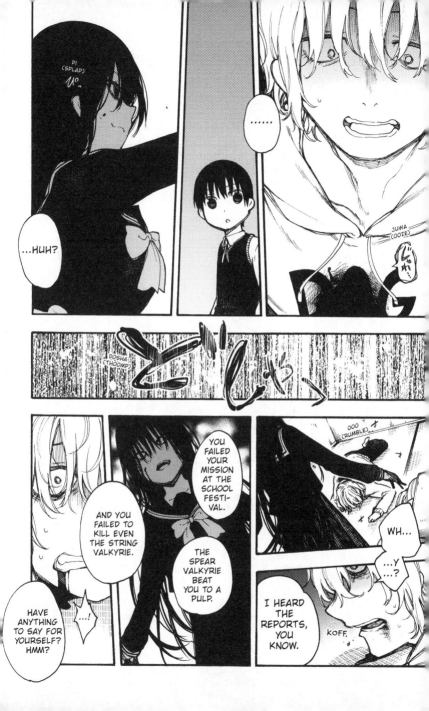

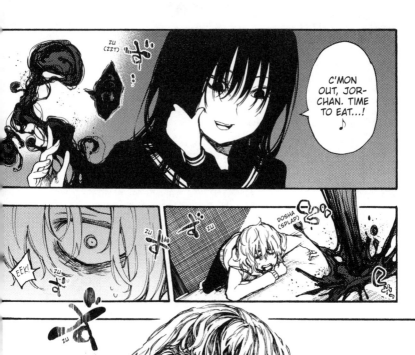

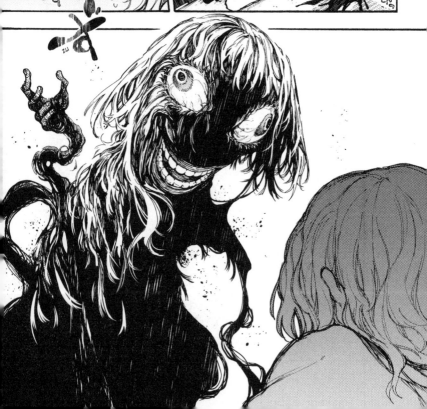

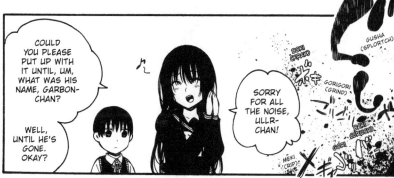

COULD YOU PLEASE PUT UP WITH IT UNTIL, UM, WHAT WAS HIS NAME, GARBON-CHAN?

WELL, UNTIL HE'S GONE. OKAY?

SORRY FOR ALL THE NOISE, ULLR-CHAN!

GUSHA (SPLORTCH)

GORIGORI (GRIND)

BAKI (CRUSH)

GORI (GORI)

MEKI (RIP)

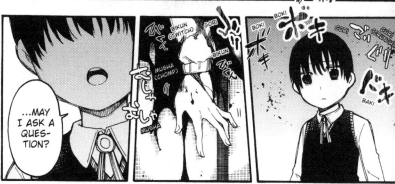

...MAY I ASK A QUES-TION?

BIKUN (TWITCH)

GORI

MUSHA (CHOMP)

BIKUN

MUSHA

BOKI

BOKI

GORI

GURI (SCRUNCH)

BAKI

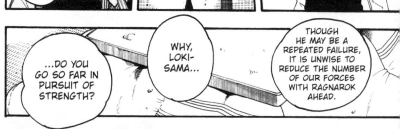

...DO YOU GO SO FAR IN PURSUIT OF STRENGTH?

WHY, LOKI-SAMA...

THOUGH HE MAY BE A REPEATED FAILURE, IT IS UNWISE TO REDUCE THE NUMBER OF OUR FORCES WITH RAGNAROK AHEAD.

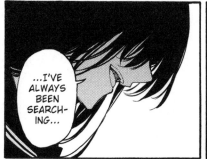

...I'VE ALWAYS BEEN SEARCH-ING...

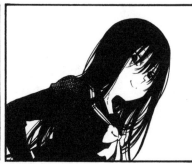

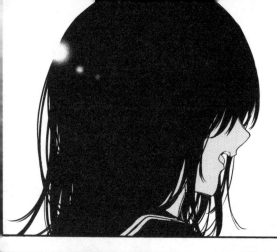
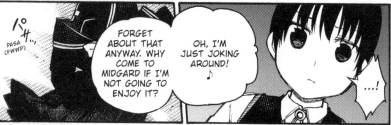
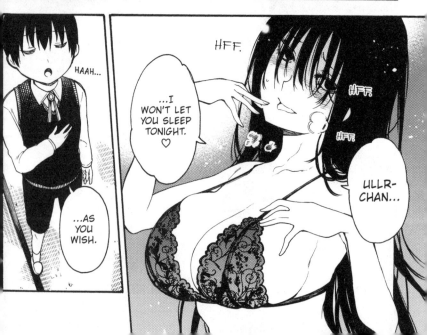

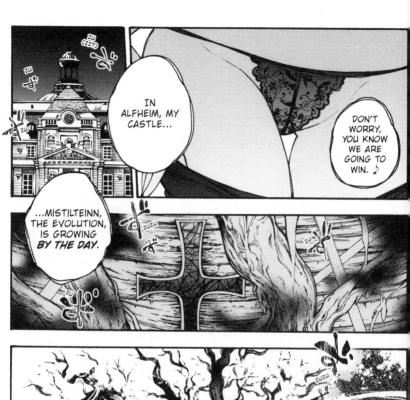

IN ALFHEIM, MY CASTLE...

DON'T WORRY, YOU KNOW WE ARE GOING TO WIN. ♪

...MISTILTEINN, THE EVOLUTION, IS GROWING *BY THE DAY.*

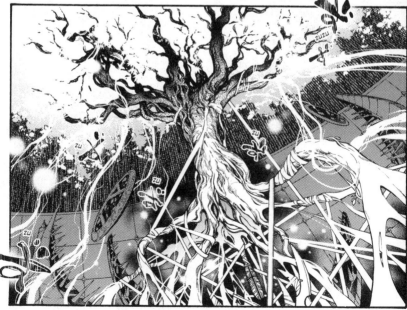

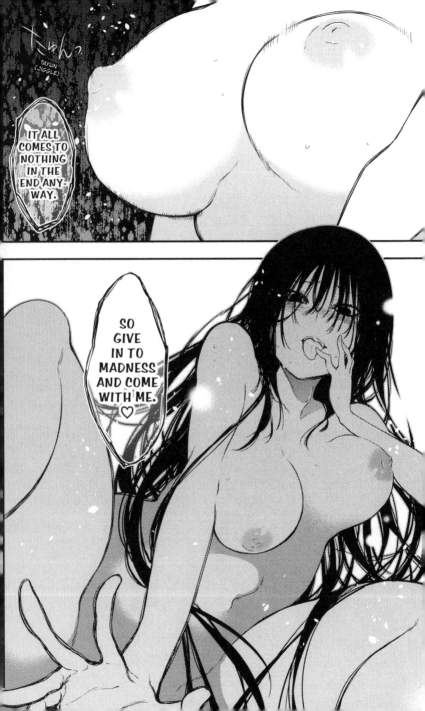

Val X Love

THERE MIGHT'VE BEEN A PLOT THAT NEVER SAW THE LIGHT OF DAY WHERE THE SISTERS COME TO EAT AT A RESTAURANT WHERE INUKAI WORKS PART-TIME.
REST IN PEACE.

ONE ORDER OF FRIED CHICKEN!

CHAKI
(CHAKK)

PIKI
(SNAP)

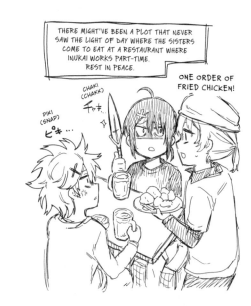

Chapter 59

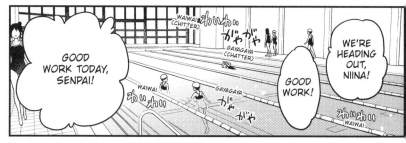

GOOD WORK TODAY, SENPAI!

WAIWAI (CHITTER)

GAYAGAYA (CHATTER)

WE'RE HEADING OUT, NIINA!

GOOD WORK!

WAIWAI

GAYAGAYA

WAIWAI

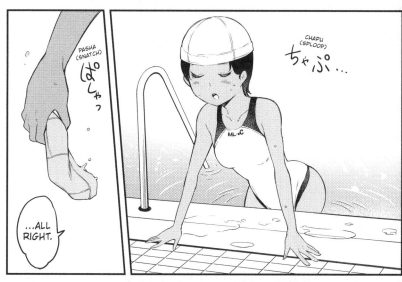

PASHA (SNATCH)

CHAPU (SPLOOP)

...ALL RIGHT.

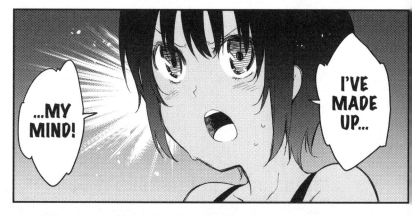

...MY MIND!

I'VE MADE UP...

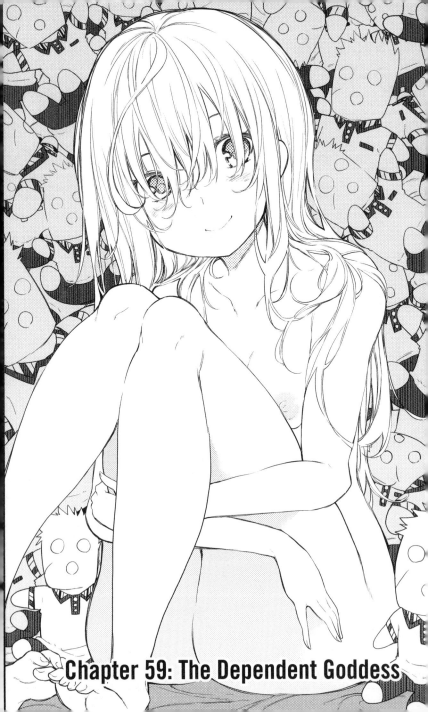

Chapter 59: The Dependent Goddess

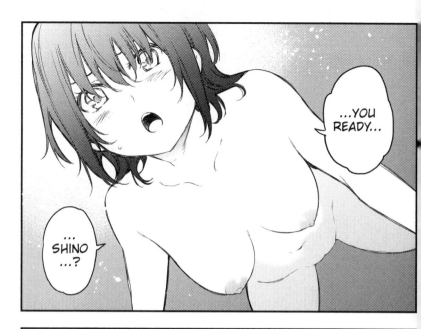

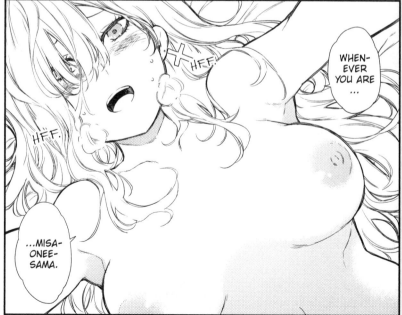

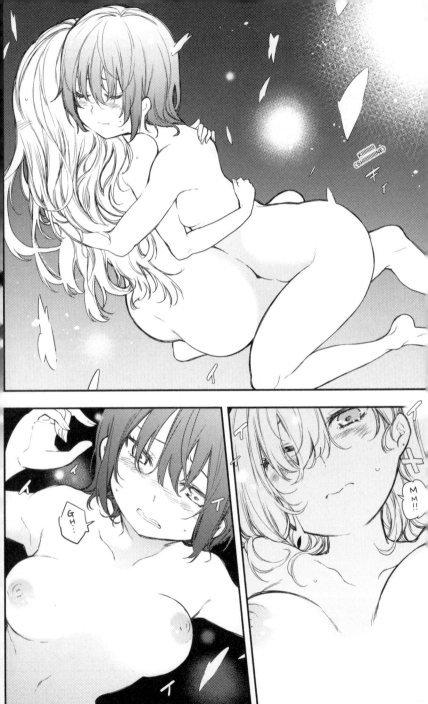

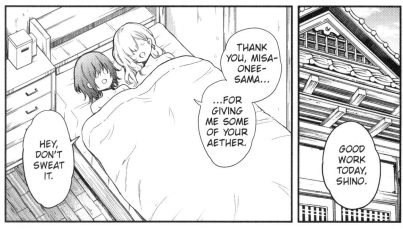

THANK YOU, MISA-ONEE-SAMA...

...FOR GIVING ME SOME OF YOUR AETHER.

HEY, DON'T SWEAT IT.

GOOD WORK TODAY, SHINO.

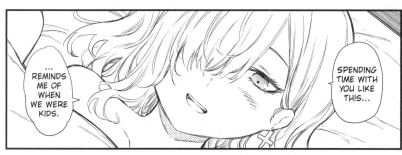

...REMINDS ME OF WHEN WE WERE KIDS.

SPENDING TIME WITH YOU LIKE THIS...

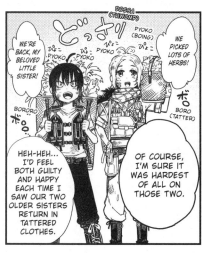

DOSSA (THWOMP)

PYOKO (BOING)

PYOKO

PYOKO

PYOKO

WE PICKED LOTS OF HERBS!

WE'RE BACK, MY BELOVED LITTLE SISTER!

BORORO

BORO (TATTER)

HEH-HEH... I'D FEEL BOTH GUILTY AND HAPPY EACH TIME I SAW OUR TWO OLDER SISTERS RETURN IN TATTERED CLOTHES.

OF COURSE, I'M SURE IT WAS HARDEST OF ALL ON THOSE TWO.

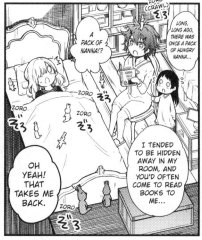

ZORO (CRAWL)

LONG, LONG AGO, THERE WAS ONCE A PACK OF HUNGRY NANNA...

A PACK OF NANNA!?

NANNA TALES

ZORO

ZORO

ZORO

ZORO

OH YEAH! THAT TAKES ME BACK.

I TENDED TO BE HIDDEN AWAY IN MY ROOM, AND YOU'D OFTEN COME TO READ BOOKS TO ME...

ZORO

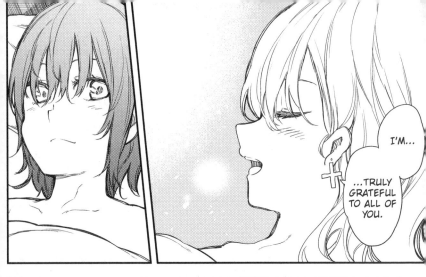

I'M...

...TRULY GRATEFUL TO ALL OF YOU.

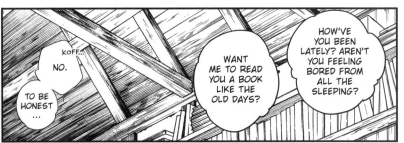

KOFF...

NO.

TO BE HONEST...

WANT ME TO READ YOU A BOOK LIKE THE OLD DAYS?

HOW'VE YOU BEEN LATELY? AREN'T YOU FEELING BORED FROM ALL THE SLEEPING?

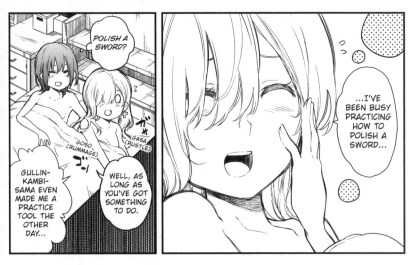

POLISH A SWORD?

GOSO (RUMMAGE)

GASA (RUSTLE)

GULLIN-KAMBI-SAMA EVEN MADE ME A PRACTICE TOOL THE OTHER DAY...

WELL, AS LONG AS YOU'VE GOT SOMETHING TO DO.

...I'VE BEEN BUSY PRACTICING HOW TO POLISH A SWORD...

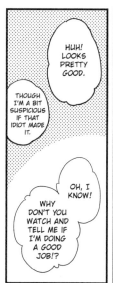

HUH! LOOKS PRETTY GOOD.

THOUGH I'M A BIT SUSPICIOUS IF THAT IDIOT MADE IT.

OH, I KNOW!

WHY DON'T YOU WATCH AND TELL ME IF I'M DOING A GOOD JOB!?

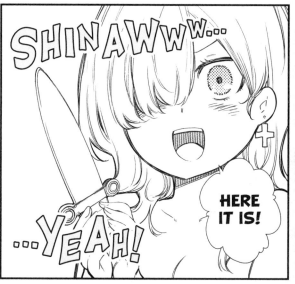

SHINAWWW...

...YEAH!

HERE IT IS!

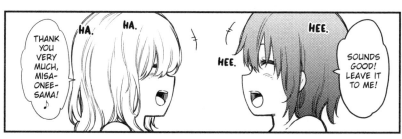

THANK YOU VERY MUCH, MISA-ONEE-SAMA!

HA. HA.

HEE. HEE.

SOUNDS GOOD! LEAVE IT TO ME!

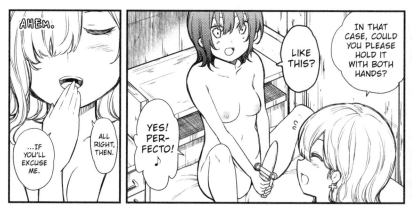

AHEM.

...IF YOU'LL EXCUSE ME.

ALL RIGHT, THEN.

LIKE THIS?

YES! PER-FECTO!

IN THAT CASE, COULD YOU PLEASE HOLD IT WITH BOTH HANDS?

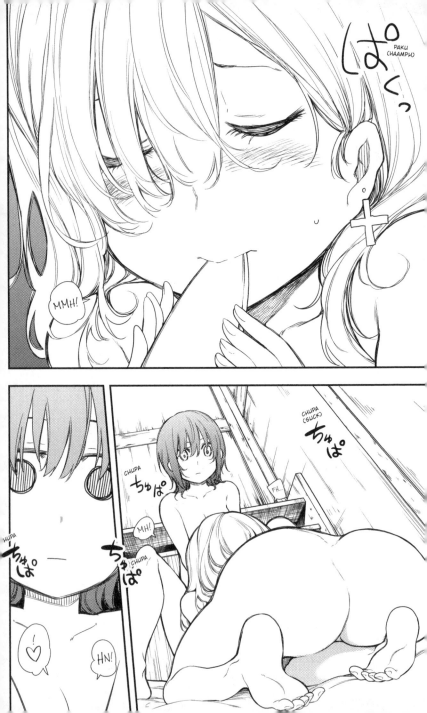

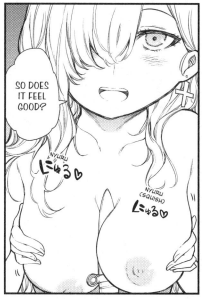

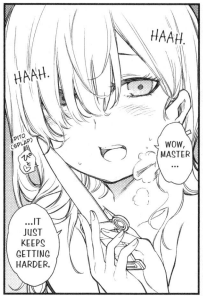

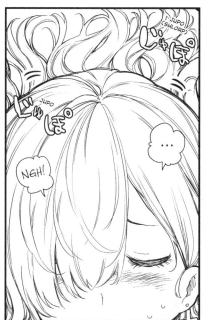

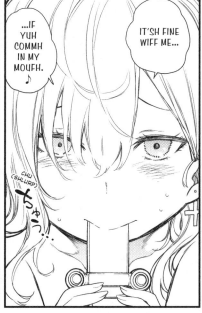

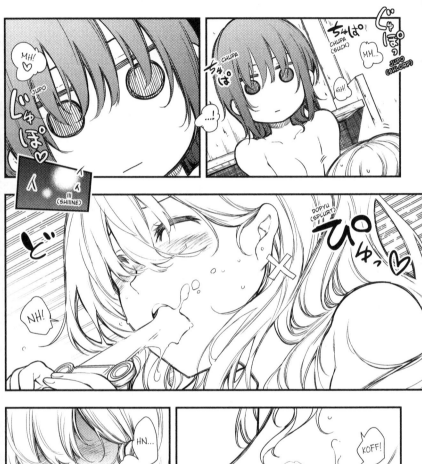

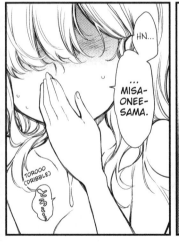

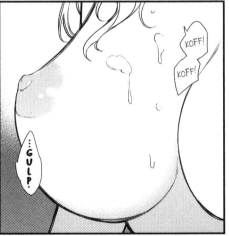

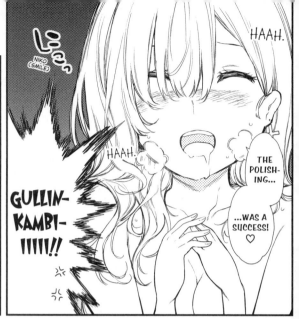

JUST AS A NOTE, THE WHITE LIQUID THAT CAME OUT AT THE END... ...IS A NUTRIENT-FILLED MILK WHICH ONLY EXCRETES IF THE CLEANING PROCESS IS A SUCCESS.

OKAY! YEAH, I GET IT!

NIKO (SMILE)

HAAH.

HAAH.

THE POLISH-ING...

...WAS A SUCCESS! ♥

GULLIN-KAMBI-IIIII!!

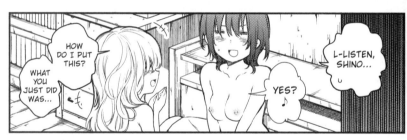

HOW DO I PUT THIS?

WHAT YOU JUST DID WAS...

L-LISTEN, SHINO...

YES? ♪

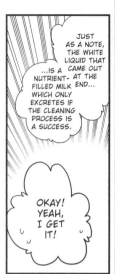

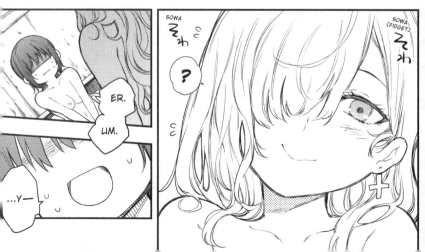

ER.

UM.

...Y—

SOWA

SOWA (FIDGET)

?

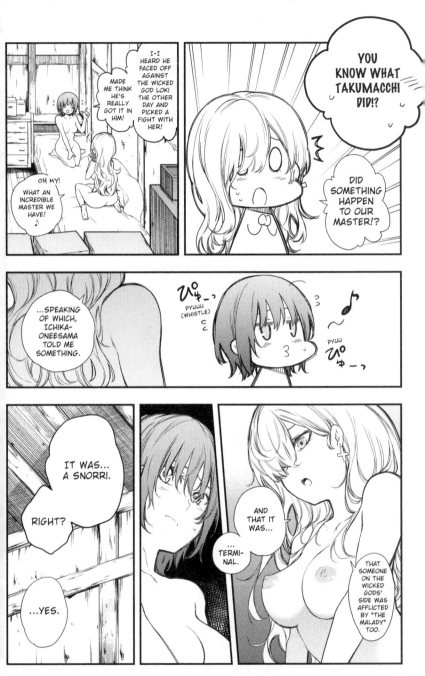

MADE ME THINK HE'S REALLY GOT IT IN HIM!

I-I HEARD HE FACED OFF AGAINST THE WICKED GOD LOKI THE OTHER DAY AND PICKED A FIGHT WITH HER!

YOU KNOW WHAT TAKUMACCHI DID!?

DID SOMETHING HAPPEN TO OUR MASTER!?

OH MY! WHAT AN INCREDIBLE MASTER WE HAVE!

...SPEAKING OF WHICH, ICHIKA-ONEESAMA TOLD ME SOMETHING.

PYUUU (WHISTLE)

PYUU

IT WAS... A SNORRI.

RIGHT?

...YES.

AND THAT IT WAS...

...TERMI-NAL.

THAT SOMEONE ON THE WICKED GODS' SIDE WAS AFFLICTED BY "THE MALADY" TOO.

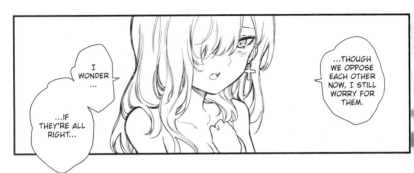

I WONDER...

...IF THEY'RE ALL RIGHT...

...THOUGH WE OPPOSE EACH OTHER NOW, I STILL WORRY FOR THEM.

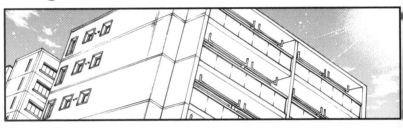

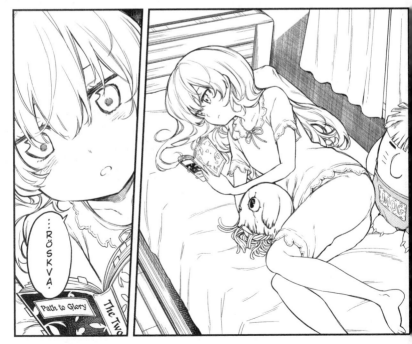

...RÖSKVA.

Path to Glory

The Two

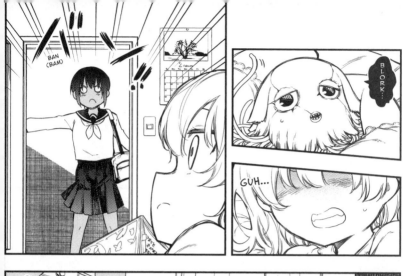

BAN
(BAM)

BLORK...

GUH...

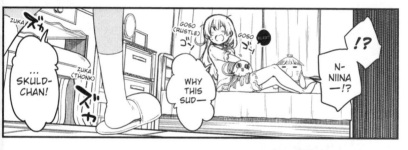

ZUKA

...SKULD-
CHAN!

ZUKA
(THONK)

GOSO
(RUSTLE)

GOSO

BLRF

WHY
THIS
SUD—

!?

N-
NIINA
—!?

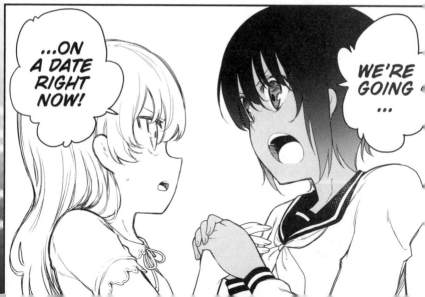

...ON
A DATE
RIGHT
NOW!

WE'RE
GOING
...

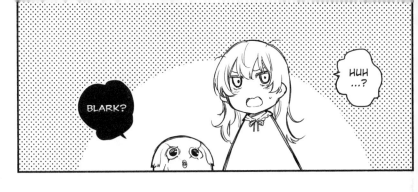

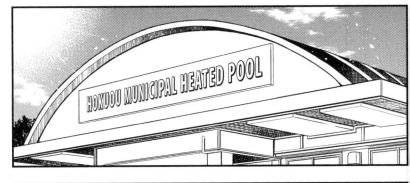

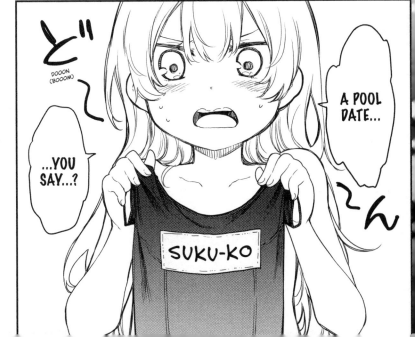

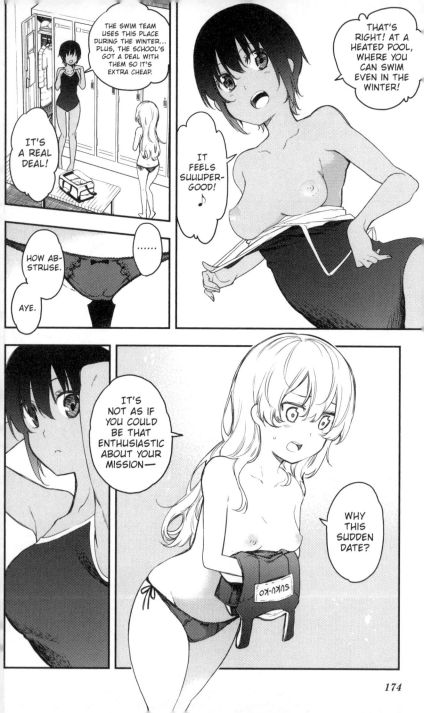

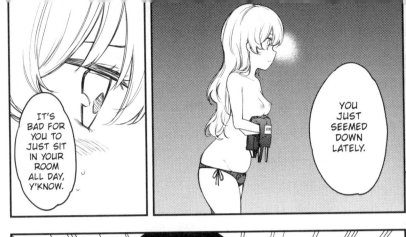

IT'S BAD FOR YOU TO JUST SIT IN YOUR ROOM ALL DAY, Y'KNOW.

YOU JUST SEEMED DOWN LATELY.

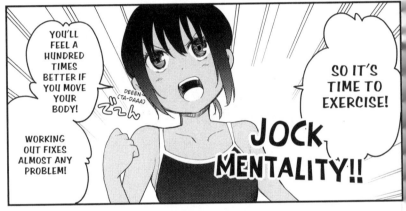

YOU'LL FEEL A HUNDRED TIMES BETTER IF YOU MOVE YOUR BODY!

WORKING OUT FIXES ALMOST ANY PROBLEM!

DEEEN (TA-DAAA)
ごこん

SO IT'S TIME TO EXERCISE!

JOCK MENTALITY!!

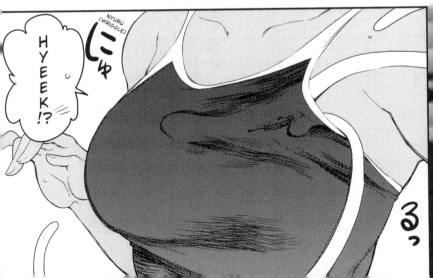

HYEEK!?

NYURU (WRIGGLE)
にゅ

る？

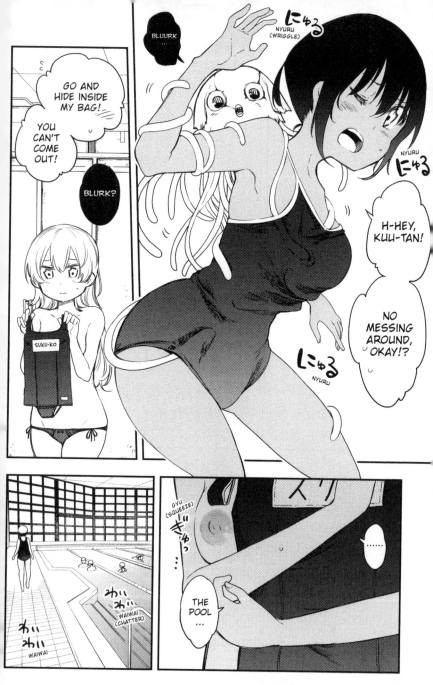

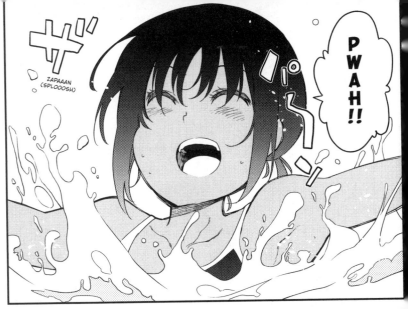

ZAPAAAN
(SPLOOOSH)

P
W
A
H
!!

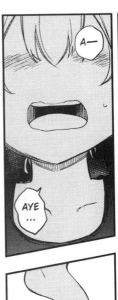

A—

AYE
...

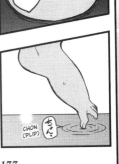

CHON
(PLIP)

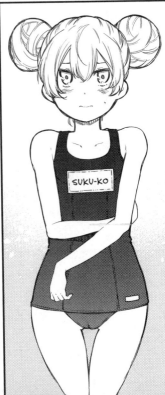

SUKU-KO

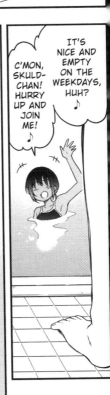

C'MON,
SKULD-
CHAN!
HURRY
UP AND
JOIN
ME!

IT'S
NICE AND
EMPTY
ON THE
WEEKDAYS,
HUH? ♪

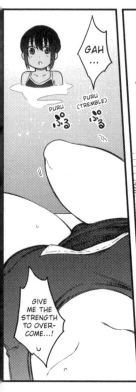

GAH...

PURU
PURU
(TREMBLE)

GIVE ME THE STRENGTH TO OVER-COME...!

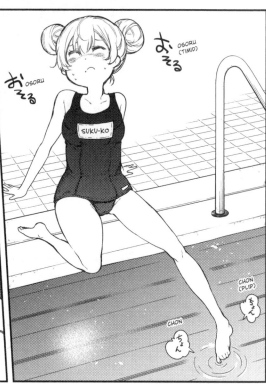

OSORU
(TIMID)

OSORU

SUKU-KO

CHON
(PLIP)

CHON

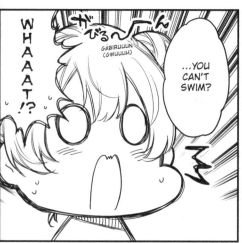

WHAAAT!?

GABIRUUUN
(GWUUUH)

...YOU CAN'T SWIM?

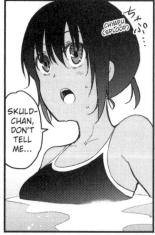

CHYAPU
(SPLOOP)

SKULD-CHAN, DON'T TELL ME...

178

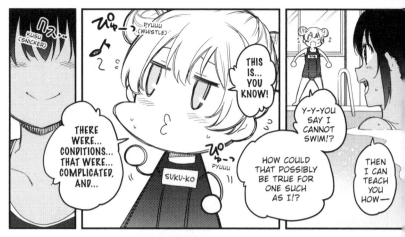
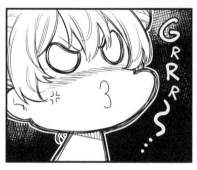
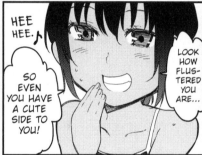
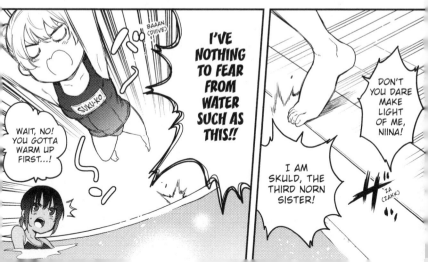

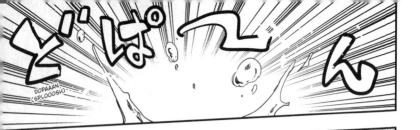

DOPAAAN
(SPLOOOSH)

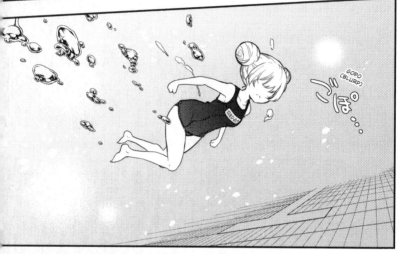

GOPO
(BLURP)

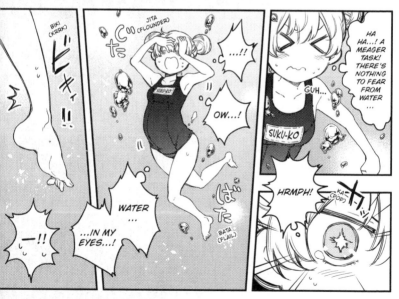

BIKI
(KRRK)

JITA
(FLOUNDER)

...!!

OW...!

WATER
...

...IN MY
EYES...!

—!!

HA
HA...! A
MEAGER
TASK!
THERE'S
NOTHING
TO FEAR
FROM
WATER
...

GUH...

SUKU-KO

HRMPH!

KA
(CROP)

BATA
(FLAIL)

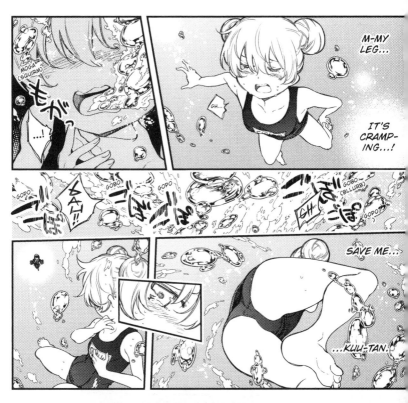

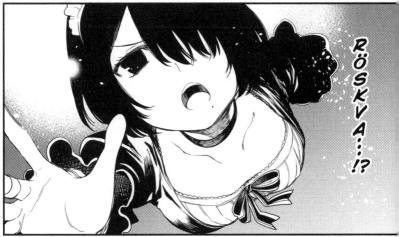

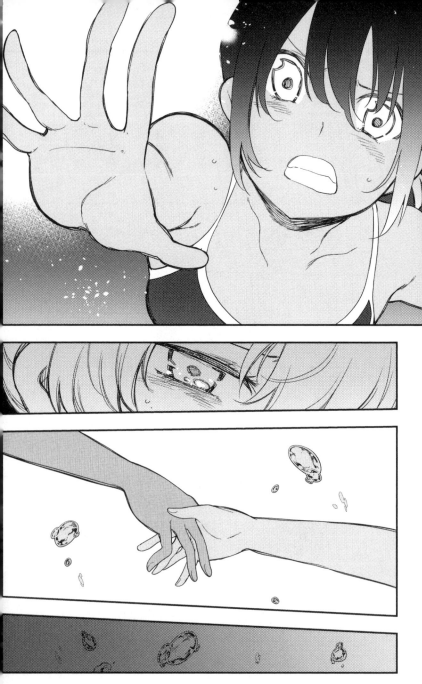

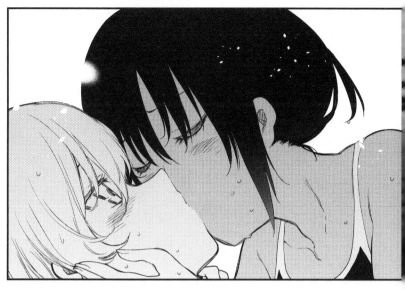

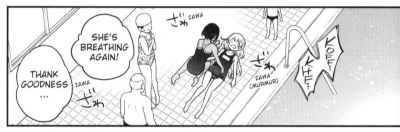

THANK GOODNESS...

SHE'S BREATHING AGAIN!

ZAWA

ZAWA (MURMUR)

ZAWA

KOFF... KHF...

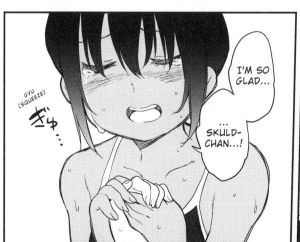

GYU (SQUEEZE)

I'M SO GLAD...

...SKULD-CHAN...!

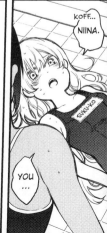

KOFF... NIINA.

YOU...

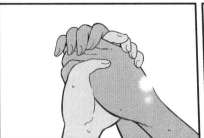

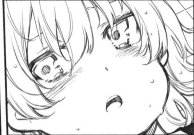

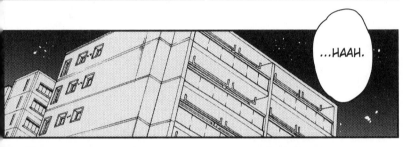

...HAAH.

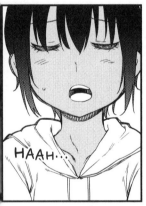

HAAH...

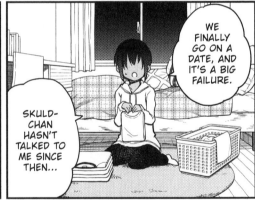

SKULD-CHAN HASN'T TALKED TO ME SINCE THEN...

WE FINALLY GO ON A DATE, AND IT'S A BIG FAILURE.

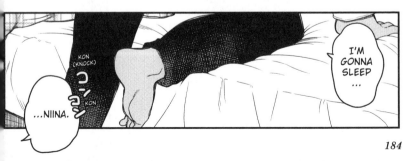

I'M GONNA SLEEP...

KON
(KNOCK)

KON

...NIINA.

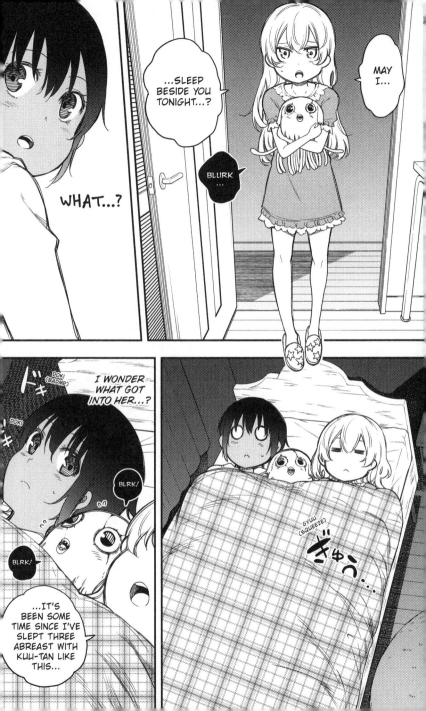

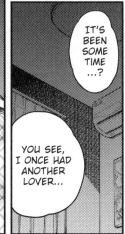

RÖSKVA...

...WAS HER NAME.

BLURK...

IT'S BEEN SOME TIME...?

YOU SEE, I ONCE HAD ANOTHER LOVER...

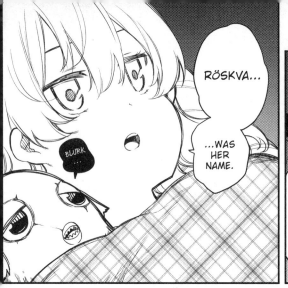

I'VE BEEN HUNTED EVER SINCE I WAS YOUNG.

THE CIR-CUMSTANCES OF MY BIRTH WERE RATHER SPECIAL, YOU SEE.

RÖSKVA-SAN...

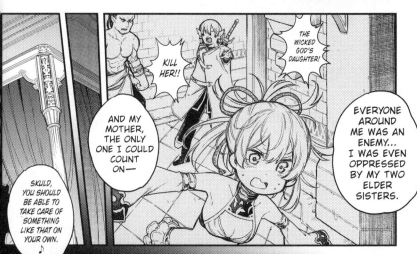

KILL HER!!

THE WICKED GOD'S DAUGHTER!

SKULD, YOU SHOULD BE ABLE TO TAKE CARE OF SOMETHING LIKE THAT ON YOUR OWN. ♪

AND MY MOTHER, THE ONLY ONE I COULD COUNT ON—

EVERYONE AROUND ME WAS AN ENEMY... I WAS EVEN OPPRESSED BY MY TWO ELDER SISTERS.

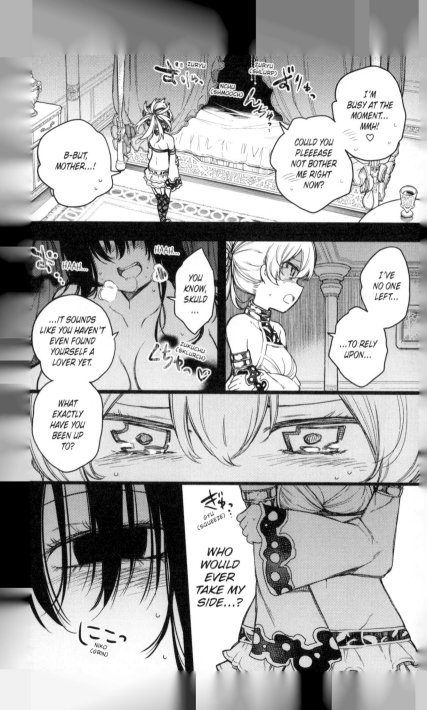

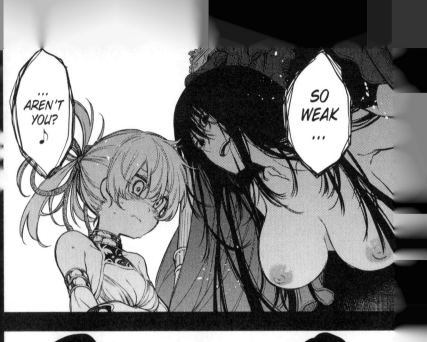

... AREN'T YOU? ♪

SO WEAK...

...EVERYTHING ABOUT YOU.

...YOUR BODY...

YOUR WILL...

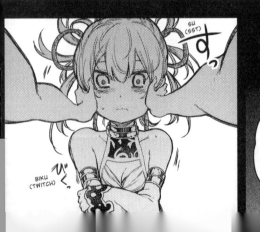

SU (SST)

BIKU (TWITCH)

AS MY DAUGHTER, YOU NEED TO BECOME STRONGER.

SO STRONG, YOU COULD KILL ME.

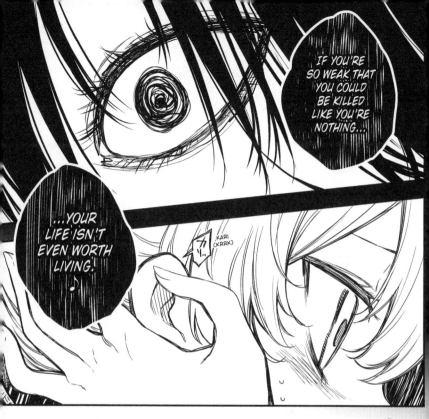

IF YOU'RE SO WEAK THAT YOU COULD BE KILLED LIKE YOU'RE NOTHING...

...YOUR LIFE ISN'T EVEN WORTH LIVING.

KARI
(KRRK)

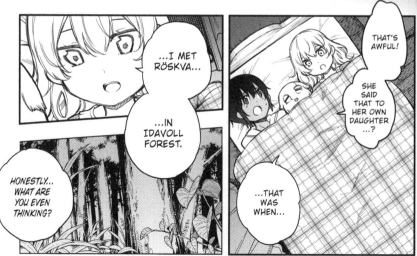

...I MET RÖSKVA...

...IN IDAVOLL FOREST.

HONESTLY... WHAT ARE YOU EVEN THINKING?

THAT'S AWFUL!

SHE SAID THAT TO HER OWN DAUGHTER...?

...THAT WAS WHEN...

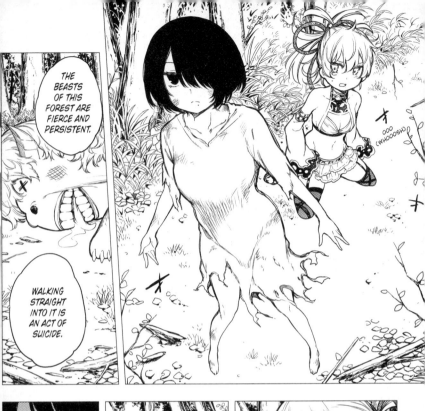

THE BEASTS OF THIS FOREST ARE FIERCE AND PERSISTENT.

WALKING STRAIGHT INTO IT IS AN ACT OF SUICIDE.

OOO (WHOOOOSH)

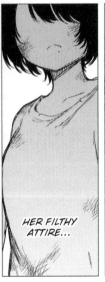

HER FILTHY ATTIRE...

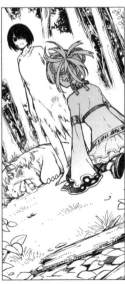

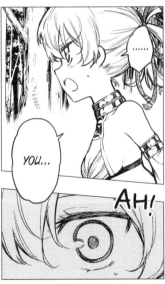

......

YOU...

AH!

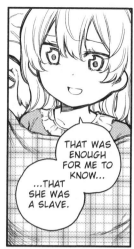

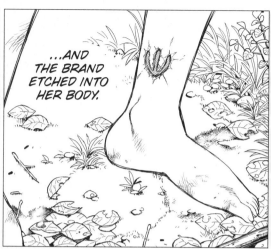

...AND THE BRAND ETCHED INTO HER BODY.

THAT WAS ENOUGH FOR ME TO KNOW...

...THAT SHE WAS A SLAVE.

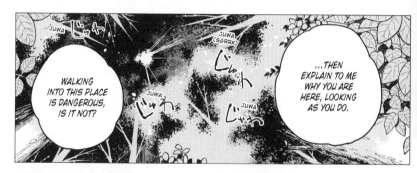

JUWA

JUWA
(SGRRK)

JUWA

JUWA

WALKING INTO THIS PLACE IS DANGEROUS, IS IT NOT?

...THEN EXPLAIN TO ME WHY YOU ARE HERE, LOOKING AS YOU DO.

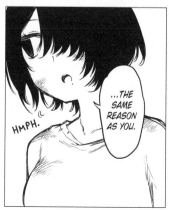

HMPH.

...THE SAME REASON AS YOU.

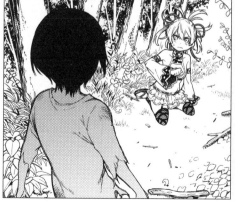

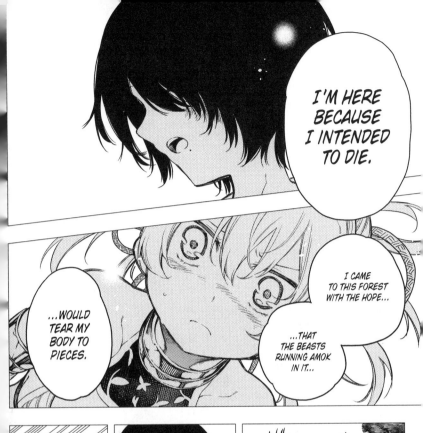

I'M HERE BECAUSE I INTENDED TO DIE.

I CAME TO THIS FOREST WITH THE HOPE...

...WOULD TEAR MY BODY TO PIECES.

...THAT THE BEASTS RUNNING AMOK IN IT...

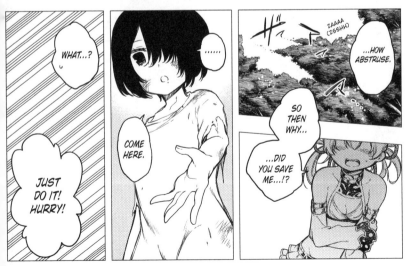

WHAT...?

JUST DO IT! HURRY!

COME HERE.

......

ZAAAA (ZSSHH)

...HOW ABSTRUSE.

SO THEN WHY...

...DID YOU SAVE ME...!?

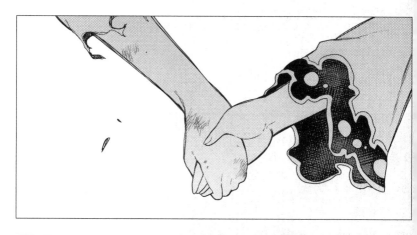

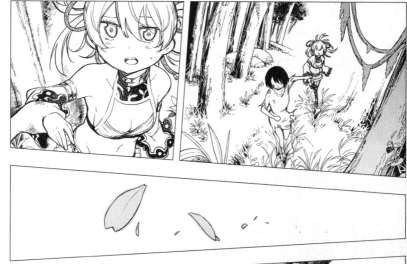

TAKE A LOOK.

THIS PLACE...

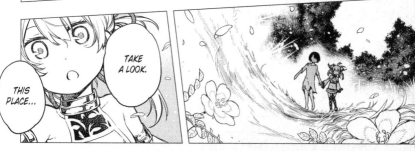

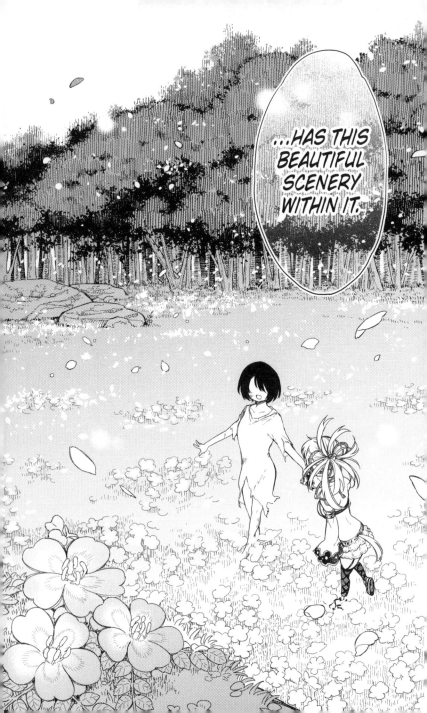

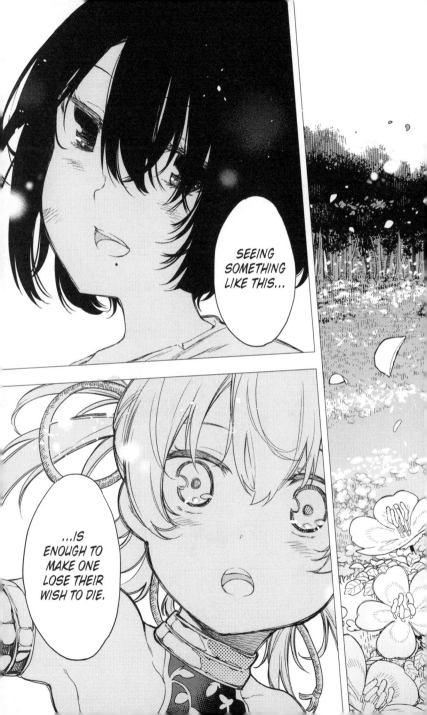

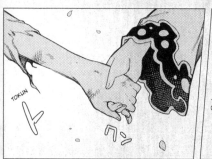

TOKUN

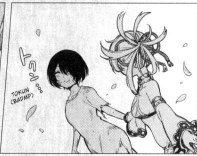

TOKUN
(BADMP)

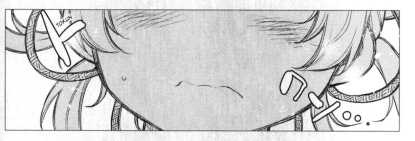

TOKUN

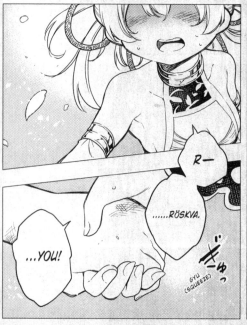

R—

......RÖSKVA.

...YOU!

GYU
(SQUEEZE)

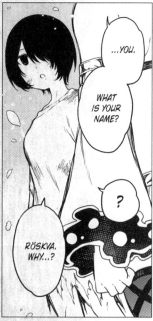

...YOU.

WHAT
IS YOUR
NAME?

?

RÖSKVA,
WHY...?

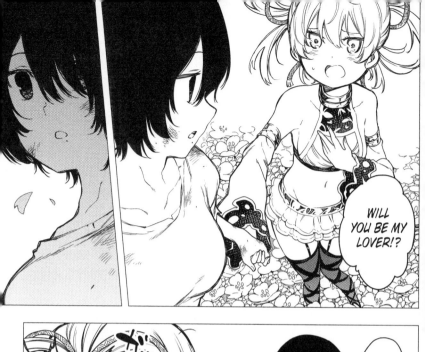

WILL YOU BE MY LOVER!?

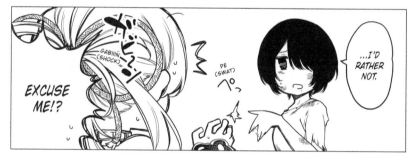

EXCUSE ME!?

GABIIIN (SHOCK)

PE (SWAT)

...I'D RATHER NOT.

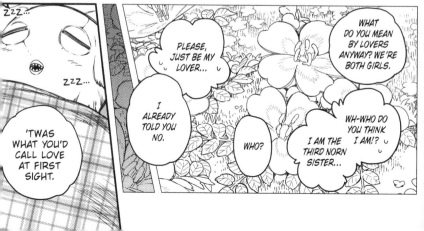

ZZZ...

ZZZ...

'TWAS WHAT YOU'D CALL LOVE AT FIRST SIGHT.

PLEASE, JUST BE MY LOVER...

I ALREADY TOLD YOU NO.

WHO?

WHAT DO YOU MEAN BY LOVERS ANYWAY? WE'RE BOTH GIRLS.

I AM THE THIRD NORN SISTER...

WH-WHO DO YOU THINK I AM!?

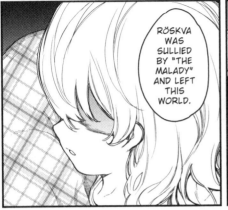

RÖSKVA WAS SULLIED BY "THE MALADY" AND LEFT THIS WORLD.

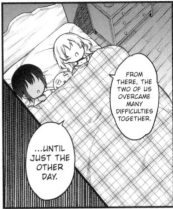

FROM THERE, THE TWO OF US OVERCAME MANY DIFFICULTIES TOGETHER.

...UNTIL JUST THE OTHER DAY.

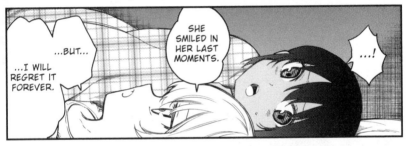

...BUT...

...I WILL REGRET IT FOREVER.

SHE SMILED IN HER LAST MOMENTS.

....!

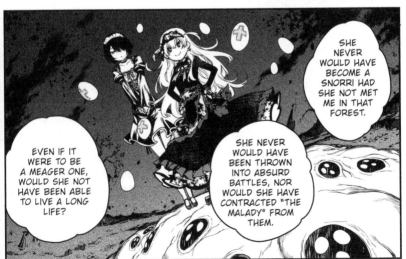

SHE NEVER WOULD HAVE BECOME A SNORRI HAD SHE NOT MET ME IN THAT FOREST.

SHE NEVER WOULD HAVE BEEN THROWN INTO ABSURD BATTLES, NOR WOULD SHE HAVE CONTRACTED "THE MALADY" FROM THEM.

EVEN IF IT WERE TO BE A MEAGER ONE, WOULD SHE NOT HAVE BEEN ABLE TO LIVE A LONG LIFE?

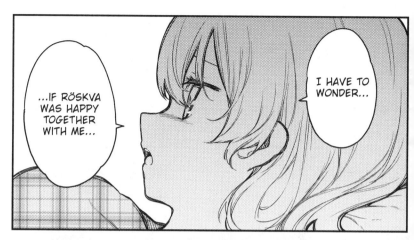

...IF RÖSKVA WAS HAPPY TOGETHER WITH ME...

I HAVE TO WONDER...

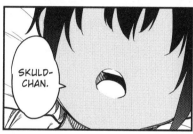

SKULD-CHAN.

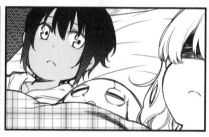

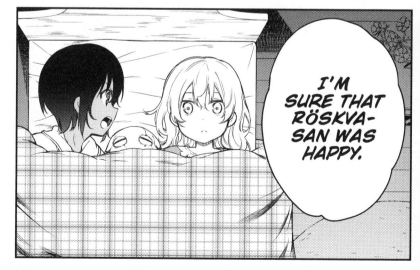

I'M SURE THAT RÖSKVA-SAN WAS HAPPY.

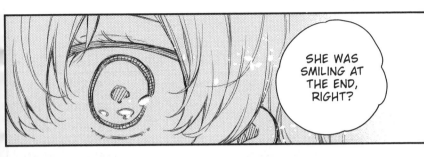

SHE WAS SMILING AT THE END, RIGHT?

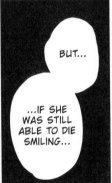

BUT...

...IF SHE WAS STILL ABLE TO DIE SMILING...

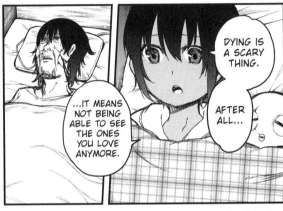

...IT MEANS NOT BEING ABLE TO SEE THE ONES YOU LOVE ANYMORE.

DYING IS A SCARY THING.

AFTER ALL...

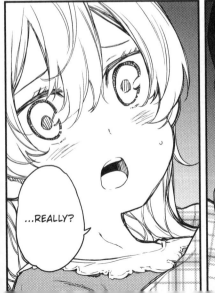

...REALLY?

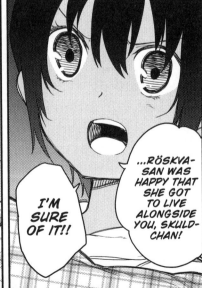

I'M SURE OF IT!!

...RÖSKVA-SAN WAS HAPPY THAT SHE GOT TO LIVE ALONGSIDE YOU, SKULD-CHAN!

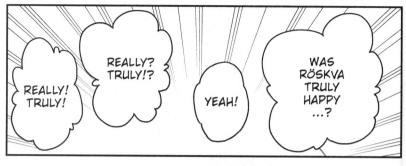

REALLY!
TRULY!

REALLY?
TRULY!?

YEAH!

WAS
RÖSKVA
TRULY
HAPPY
...?

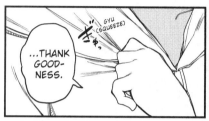

...THANK
GOOD-
NESS.

GYU
(SQUEEZE)

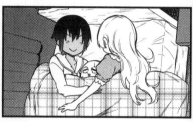

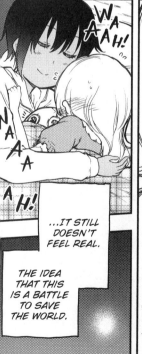

WAAAH!

NAAAAH!

...IT STILL
DOESN'T
FEEL REAL.

THE IDEA
THAT THIS
IS A BATTLE
TO SAVE
THE WORLD.

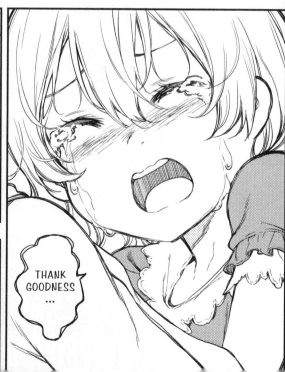

THANK
GOODNESS
...

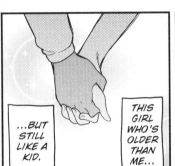

...BUT STILL LIKE A KID.

THIS GIRL WHO'S OLDER THAN ME...

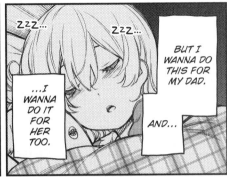

ZZZ...

ZZZ...

...I WANNA DO IT FOR HER TOO.

BUT I WANNA DO THIS FOR MY DAD.

AND...

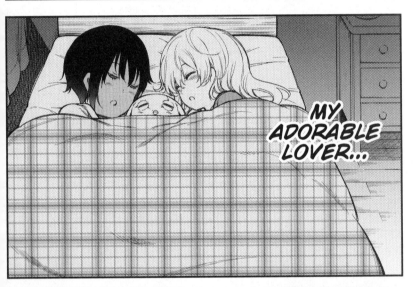

MY ADORABLE LOVER...

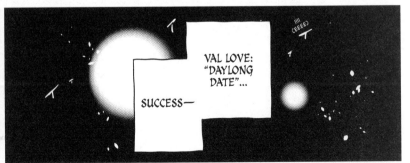

(EEEE)

VAL LOVE: "DAYLONG DATE"...

SUCCESS—

Val X Love

I WAS HAPPY.

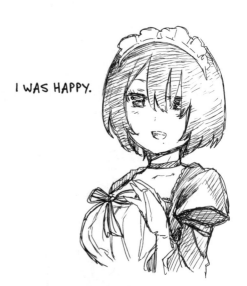

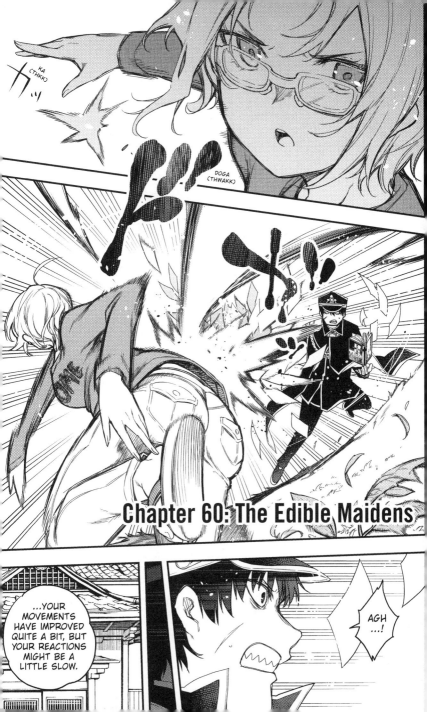

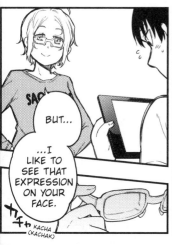

BUT...

...I LIKE TO SEE THAT EXPRESSION ON YOUR FACE.

カチャ KACHA
(KACHAK)

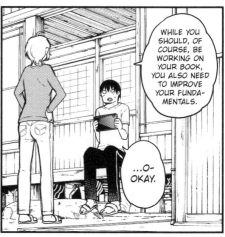

WHILE YOU SHOULD, OF COURSE, BE WORKING ON YOUR BOOK, YOU ALSO NEED TO IMPROVE YOUR FUNDA-MENTALS.

...O-OKAY.

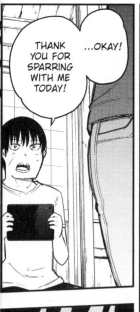

THANK YOU FOR SPARRING WITH ME TODAY!

...OKAY!

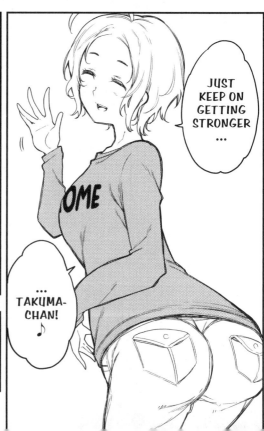

JUST KEEP ON GETTING STRONGER...

...TAKUMA-CHAN! ♪

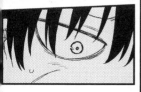

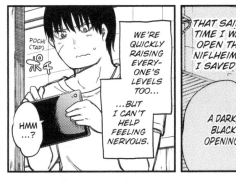

POCHI (TAP)

WE'RE QUICKLY RAISING EVERYONE'S LEVELS TOO...

...BUT I CAN'T HELP FEELING NERVOUS.

HMM...?

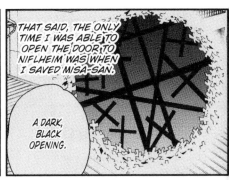

THAT SAID, THE ONLY TIME I WAS ABLE TO OPEN THE DOOR TO NIFLHEIM WAS WHEN I SAVED MISA-SAN.

A DARK, BLACK OPENING.

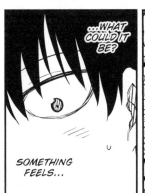

...WHAT COULD IT BE?

SOMETHING FEELS...

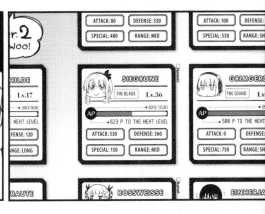

Lr.2
woo!

ATTACK: 80 | DEFENSE: 330
SPECIAL: 480 | RANGE: MID

ATTACK: 100 | DEFENSE:
SPECIAL: 530 | RANGE: SH

HILDE
Lv.17
380/990
NEHT LEVEL
EFENSE: 120
ANGE: LONG

SIEGRUNE
THE BLADE | Lv.36
AP — 820/1630
623 P TO THE NEHT LEVEL
ATTACK: 530 | DEFENSE: 360
SPECIAL: 150 | RANGE: MID

GRIMGER
THE SOUND | Lv
AP
508 P TO THE NEHT
ATTACK: 0 | DEFENSE:
SPECIAL: 750 | RANGE: SH

RAUTE

ROSSWEISSE

EINHERJA

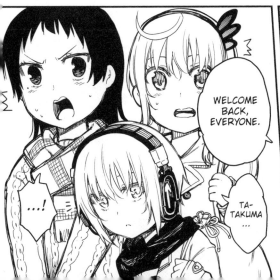

WELCOME BACK, EVERYONE.

....!

TA-TAKUMA...

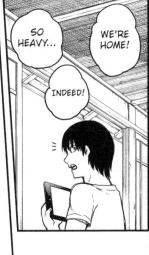

SO HEAVY...

WE'RE HOME!

INDEED!

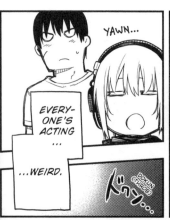

YAWN...

EVERY-ONE'S ACTING ...

...WEIRD.

DOKUN DOKUN
ドクッ ドクッ...

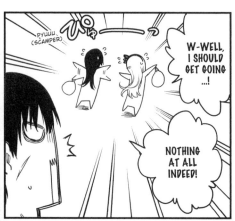

PYUUU
(SCAMPER)

W-WELL, I SHOULD GET GOING ...!

NOTHING AT ALL INDEED!

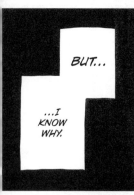

BUT...

...I KNOW WHY.

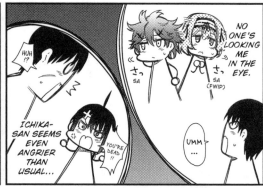

HUH !?

ICHIKA-SAN SEEMS EVEN ANGRIER THAN USUAL...

YOU'RE DEAD !!

NO ONE'S LOOKING ME IN THE EYE.

SA

SA
(FWIP)

UMM ...

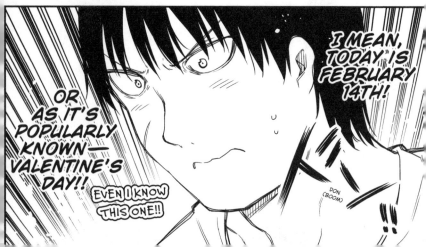

OR AS IT'S POPULARLY KNOWN— VALENTINE'S DAY!!

EVEN I KNOW THIS ONE!!

I MEAN, TODAY IS FEBRUARY 14TH!

DON
(BOOM)

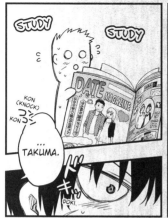

STUDY STUDY

KON (KNOCK)
KON

...TAKUMA.

DOKI

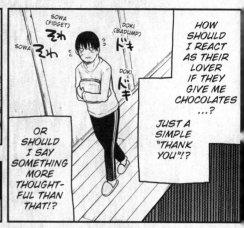

SOWA (FIDGET)
SOWA
DOKI (BADUMP)
DOKI

HOW SHOULD I REACT AS THEIR LOVER IF THEY GIVE ME CHOCOLATES...?

JUST A SIMPLE "THANK YOU"!?

OR SHOULD I SAY SOMETHING MORE THOUGHTFUL THAN THAT!?

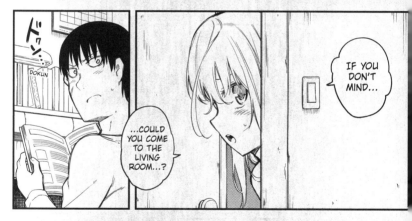

DOKIN

...COULD YOU COME TO THE LIVING ROOM...?

IF YOU DON'T MIND...

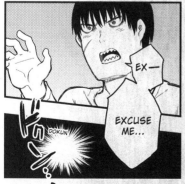

DOKUN

EX—

EXCUSE ME...

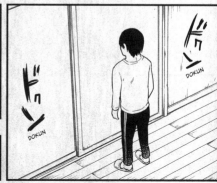

DOKUN
DOKUN

209

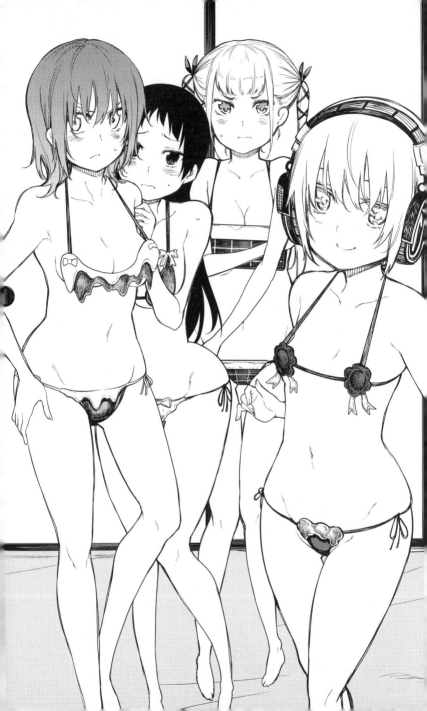

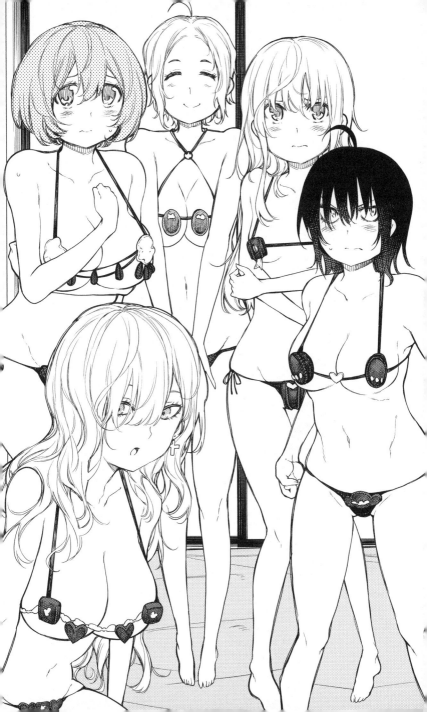

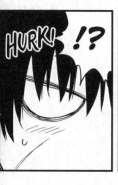

HURK! !?

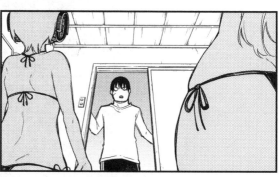

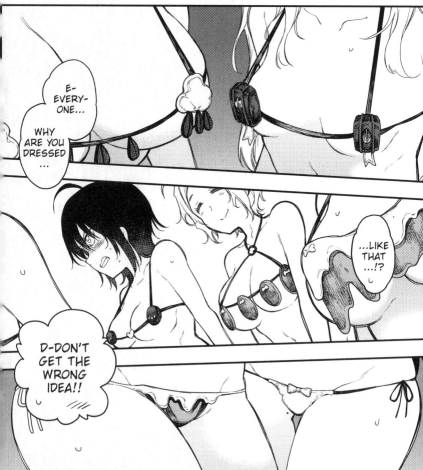

E-EVERY-ONE...

WHY ARE YOU DRESSED...

...LIKE THAT...!?

D-DON'T GET THE WRONG IDEA!!

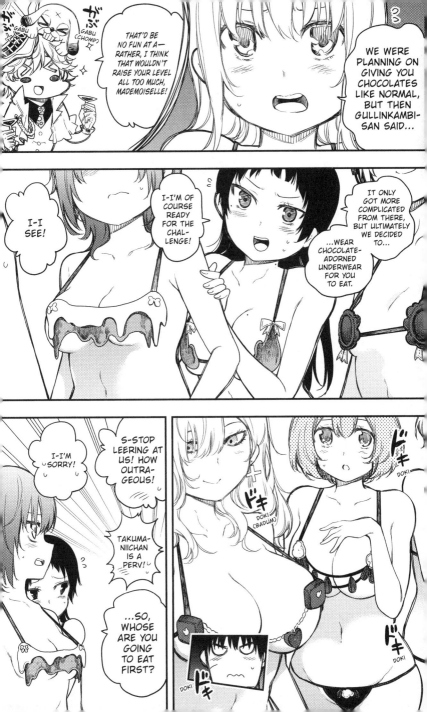

GABU

GABU (CHOMP)

THAT'D BE NO FUN AT A—RATHER, I THINK THAT WOULDN'T RAISE YOUR LEVEL ALL TOO MUCH, MADEMOISELLE!

WE WERE PLANNING ON GIVING YOU CHOCOLATES LIKE NORMAL, BUT THEN GULLINKAMBI-SAN SAID...

I-I SEE!

I-I'M OF COURSE READY FOR THE CHALLENGE!

IT ONLY GOT MORE COMPLICATED FROM THERE, BUT ULTIMATELY WE DECIDED TO...

...WEAR CHOCOLATE-ADORNED UNDERWEAR FOR YOU TO EAT.

I-I'M SORRY!

S-STOP LEERING AT US! HOW OUTRA-GEOUS!

TAKUMA-NIICHAN IS A PERV!

...SO, WHOSE ARE YOU GOING TO EAT FIRST?

DOKI

DOKI (BADUM)

DOKI

DOKI

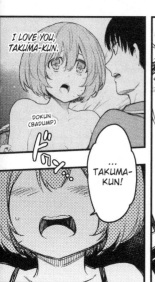

I LOVE YOU, TAKUMA-KUN.

DOKUN (BADUMP)

... TAKUMA-KUN!

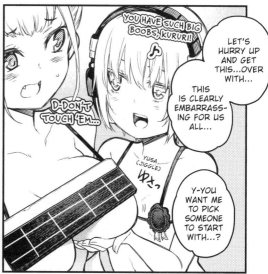

YOU HAVE SUCH BIG BOOBS, KURURI!! ♪

D-DON'T TOUCH 'EM...

LET'S HURRY UP AND GET THIS...OVER WITH...

THIS IS CLEARLY EMBARRASSING FOR US ALL...

YUSA (JIGGLE)

Y-YOU WANT ME TO PICK SOMEONE TO START WITH...?

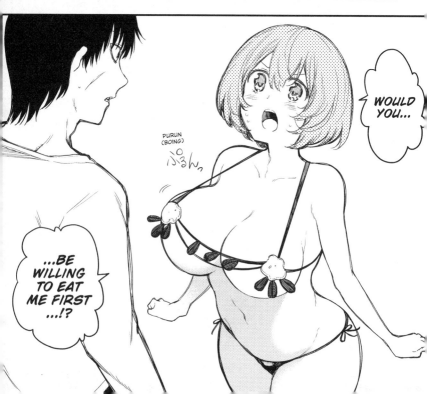

WOULD YOU...

PURUN (BOING)

...BE WILLING TO EAT ME FIRST ...!?

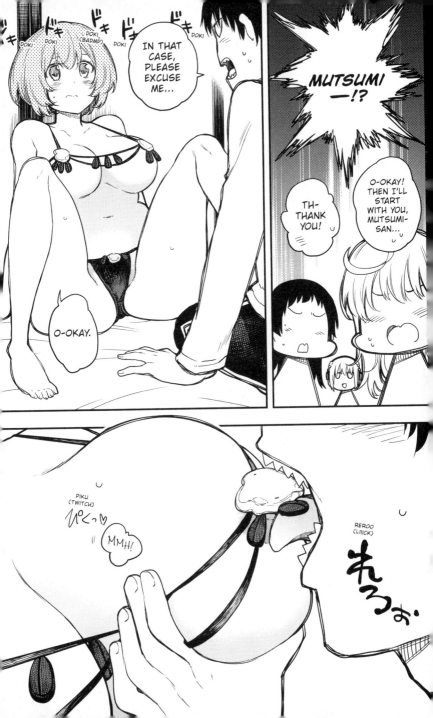

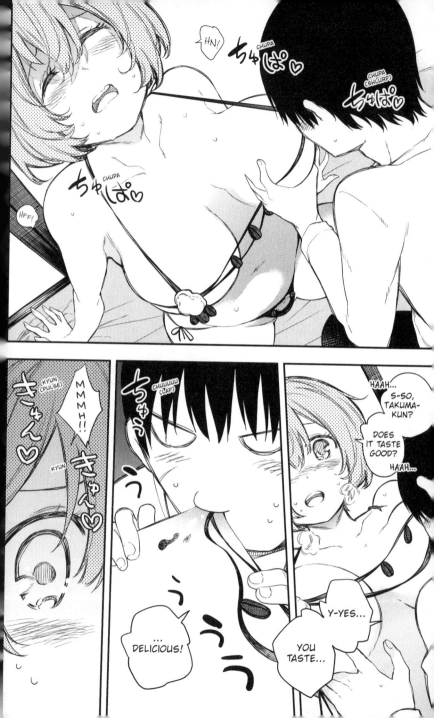

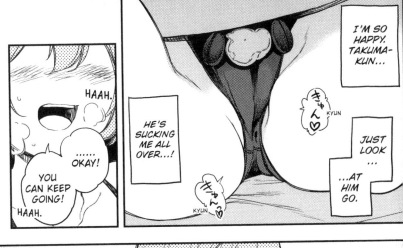

HAAH.

...... OKAY!

YOU CAN KEEP GOING!

HAAH.

HE'S SUCKING ME ALL OVER...!

I'M SO HAPPY, TAKUMA-KUN...

きゅん KYUN

JUST LOOK ...

...AT HIM GO.

きゅん KYUN

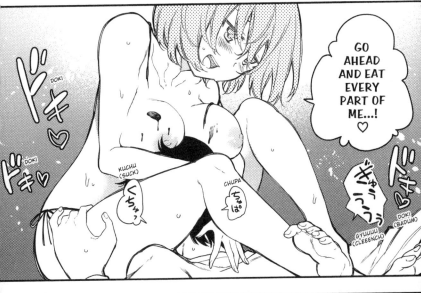

GO AHEAD AND EAT EVERY PART OF ME...! ♡

ドキ DOKI

ドキ DOKI

KUCHU (SUCK)

くちゅ

CHUPA

ちゅぱ

ぎゅうう GYUUUU (CLEEENCH)

バドゥ (DOKI) (BADUM)

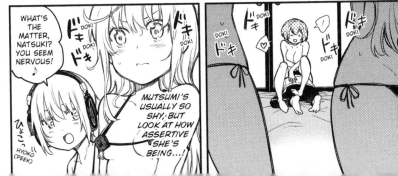

WHAT'S THE MATTER, NATSUKI? YOU SEEM NERVOUS! ♪

ドキ DOKI
ドキ DOKI
ドキ DOKI

MUTSUMI'S USUALLY SO SHY, BUT LOOK AT HOW ASSERTIVE SHE'S BEING...!

ひょこっ HYOKO (PEEK)

ドキ DOKI
ドキ DOKI
ドキ DOKI
ドキ DOKI

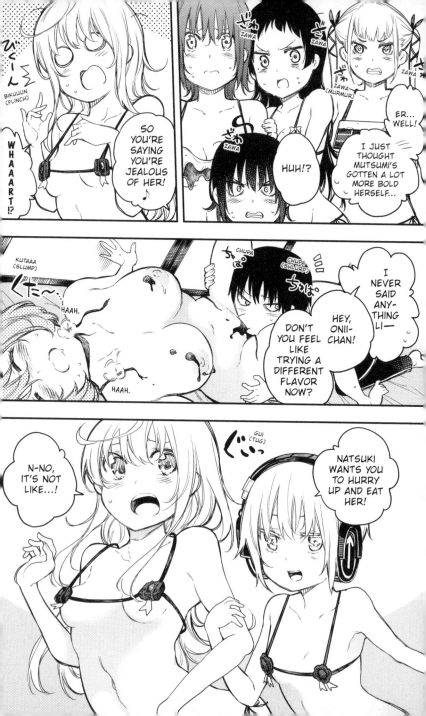

DOKUN (BADMP)

...I'M GETTING SO LIGHT-HEADED.

THE ROOM GETS EVEN MORE HEATED!

HN!

PIKU (TWITCH)

A REROO (LIIICK)

THIS CHOCOLATE IS SO YUMMY!

BUT FOR SOME REASON...

MUSHA MUSHA

AS FOR S-CHAN, SHE COULDN'T POSSIBLY BE WATCHING— SHE'S EATING CHOCOLATE IN A CORNER OF THE ROOM!

DON (BOOM)

DON

DON

DON

KEEP OUT   KEEP OUT

DON

MEANWHILE, ODIN WANTS TO SEE HIS DAUGHTERS' GROWN AND NOT-EVEN-CLOSE-TO-NUDE FIGURES!

O-OPEN UP, PLEEEE-ASE!!

BUT—

DOKUN

GARI (GRIND)

WHAT A HUNGRY BOY YOU ARE.

GARI

MY GOODNESS, TAKUMA-CHAN.

HN!

WH-WHEN WOULD BE THE RIGHT TIME TO HAVE TAKUMA-SAN EAT ME...?

M-MISA-NEESAMA!

WAKU
WAKU (GIDDY)
WAKU

D-DON'T ASK ME THAT!

WE WERE FAR TOO LATE TO MAKE OUR MOVE!!

DODEDEEEN (GUHHHH)

POIN (PWOING)

WOOF !!

EEK !?

...!?

AH!

WOOF !!

S...S-SAN?

WHAT'S GOTTEN INTO YOU ALL OF A SUDDEN?

MUSHA

MUSHA

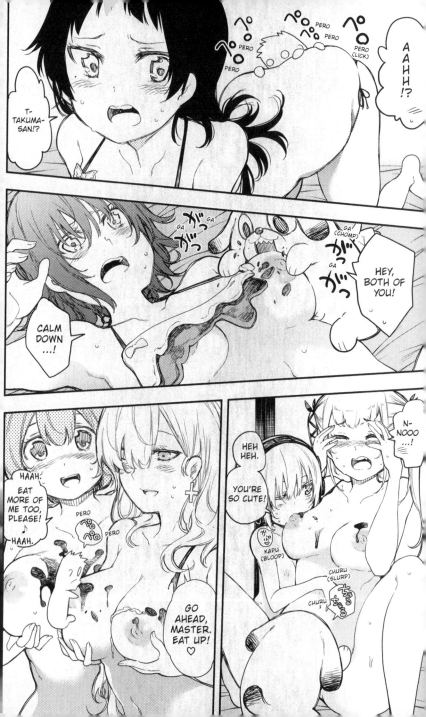

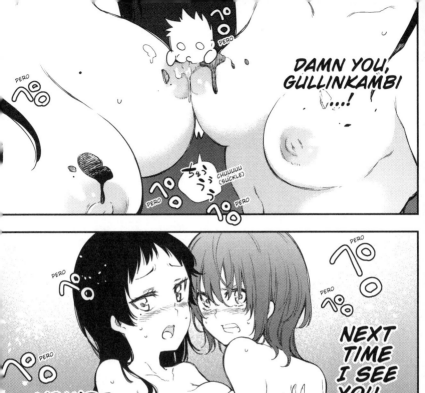
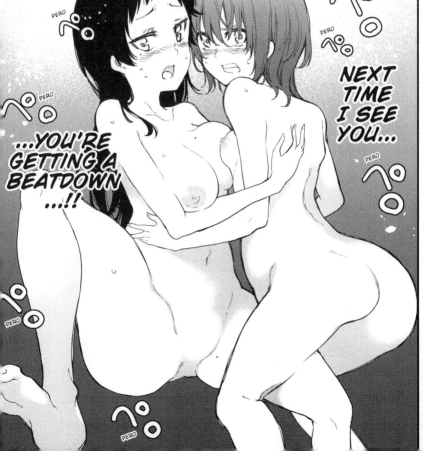

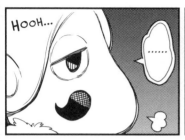

HOOH...

......

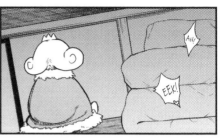

AH!

EEK!

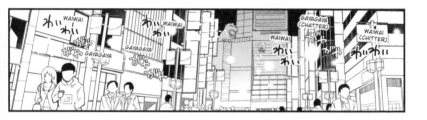

WAIWAI

WAIWAI

GAYAGAYA

GAYAGAYA

WAIWAI

GAYAGAYA
(CHATTER)

WAIWAI
(CHITTER)

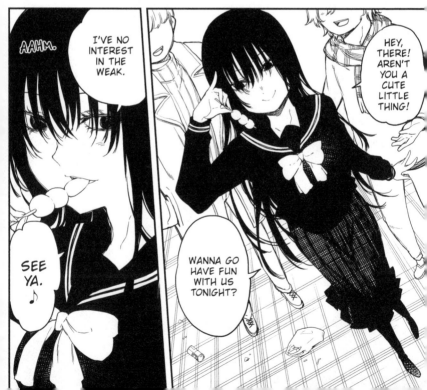

AAHM.

I'VE NO INTEREST IN THE WEAK.

SEE YA. ♪

HEY, THERE! AREN'T YOU A CUTE LITTLE THING!

WANNA GO HAVE FUN WITH US TONIGHT?

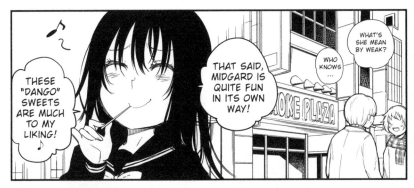

THESE "DANGO" SWEETS ARE MUCH TO MY LIKING!

THAT SAID, MIDGARD IS QUITE FUN IN ITS OWN WAY!

WHO KNOWS...

WHAT'S SHE MEAN BY WEAK?

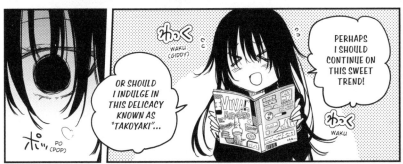

WAKU (GIDDY)

OR SHOULD I INDULGE IN THIS DELICACY KNOWN AS "TAKOYAKI"...

PO (POP)

VIVA! MIDGARD

PERHAPS I SHOULD CONTINUE ON THIS SWEET TREND!

WAKU

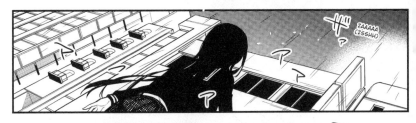

ZAAAAA (ZSSHH)

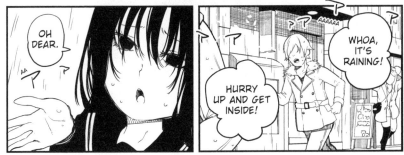

OH DEAR.

WHOA, IT'S RAINING!

HURRY UP AND GET INSIDE!

AAAAAA

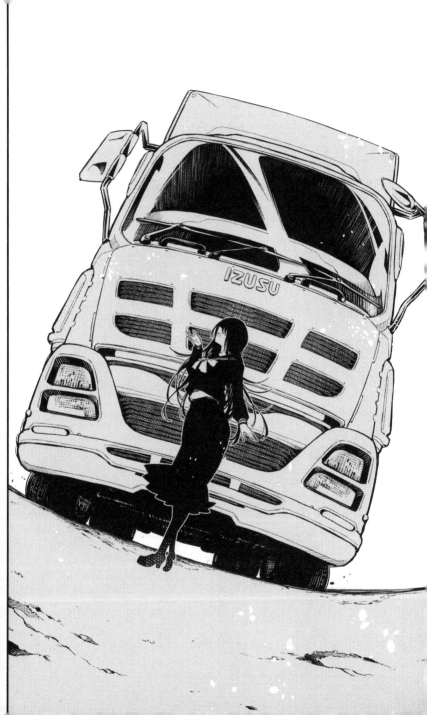

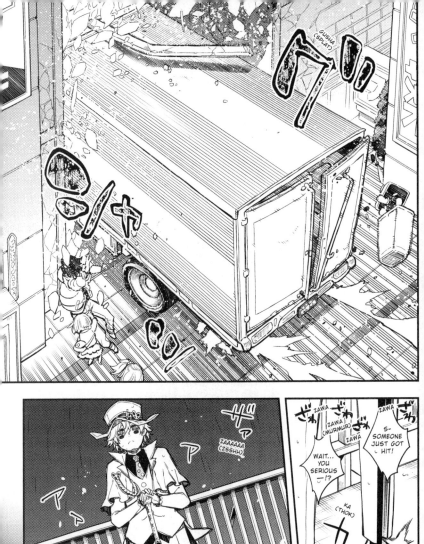

GUSHA
(SPLAT)

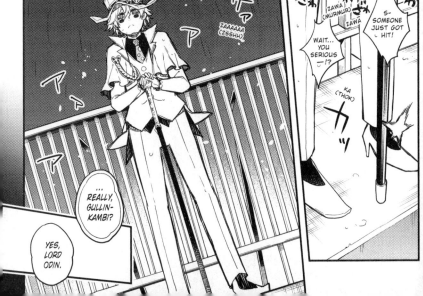

ZAAAAAA
(TSSHH)

... REALLY, GULLIN-KAMBI?

YES, LORD ODIN.

ZAWA

ZAWA
(MURMUR)

ZAWA

ZAWA

S-SOMEONE JUST GOT HIT!

WAIT... YOU SERIOUS —!?

KA
(THOK)

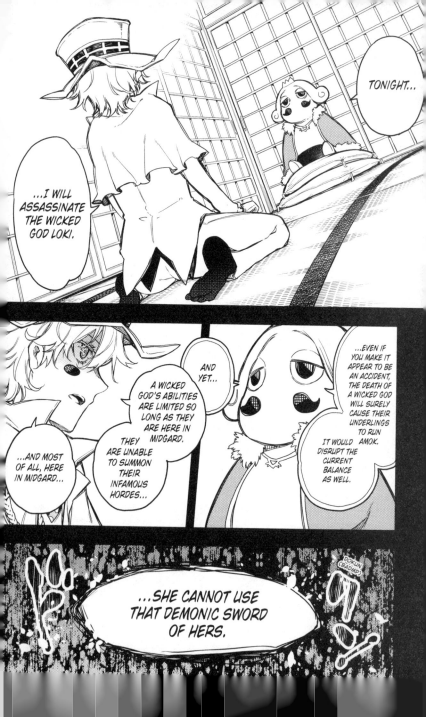

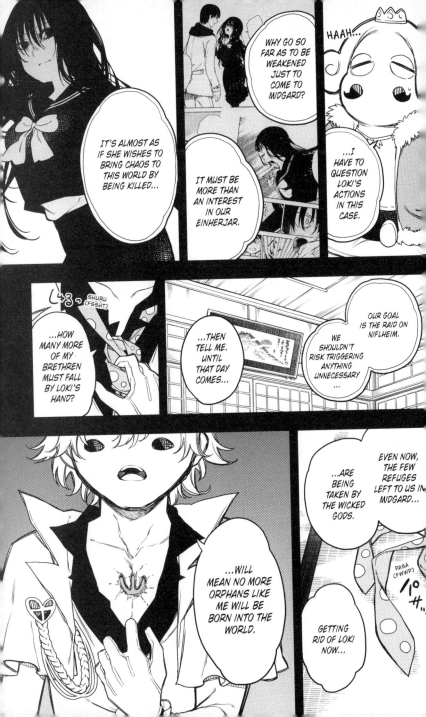

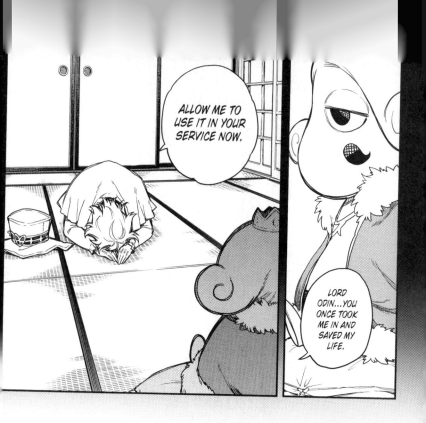

ALLOW ME TO USE IT IN YOUR SERVICE NOW.

LORD ODIN...YOU ONCE TOOK ME IN AND SAVED MY LIFE.

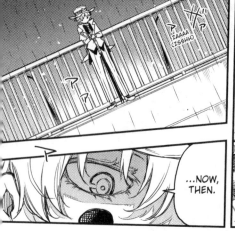

...NOW, THEN.

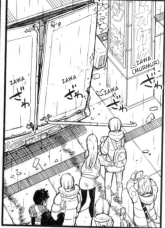

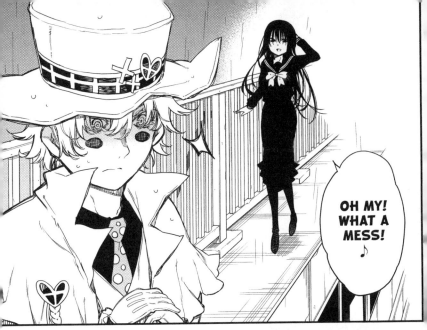

OH MY! WHAT A MESS! ♪

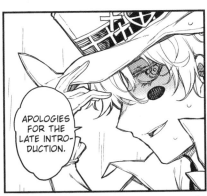

APOLOGIES FOR THE LATE INTRO-DUCTION.

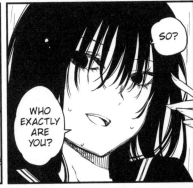

SO?

WHO EXACTLY ARE YOU?

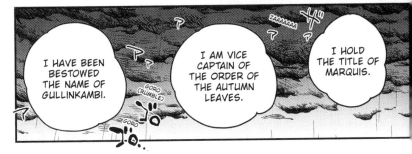

I HAVE BEEN BESTOWED THE NAME OF GULLINKAMBI.

I AM VICE CAPTAIN OF THE ORDER OF THE AUTUMN LEAVES.

I HOLD THE TITLE OF MARQUIS.

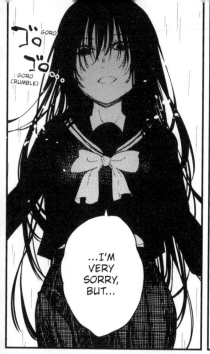

GORO

GORO
(RUMBLE)

...I'M VERY SORRY, BUT...

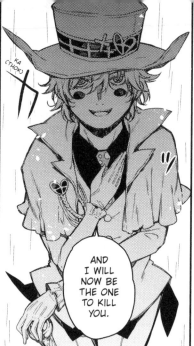

KA
(THOK)

AND I WILL NOW BE THE ONE TO KILL YOU.

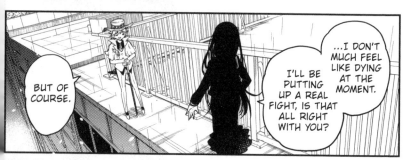

BUT OF COURSE.

I'LL BE PUTTING UP A REAL FIGHT, IS THAT ALL RIGHT WITH YOU?

...I DON'T MUCH FEEL LIKE DYING AT THE MOMENT.

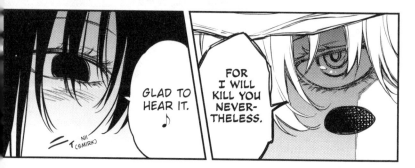

GLAD TO HEAR IT. ♪

NII
(SMIRK)

FOR I WILL KILL YOU NEVER-THELESS.

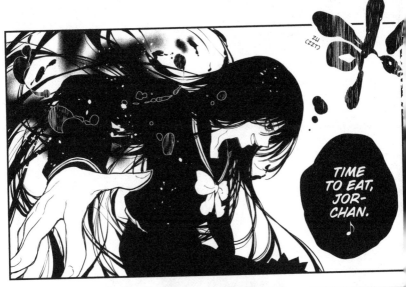

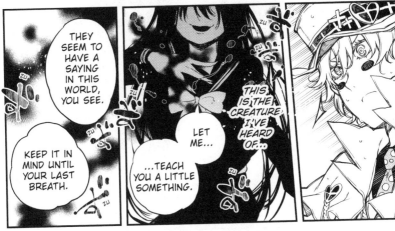

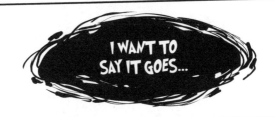

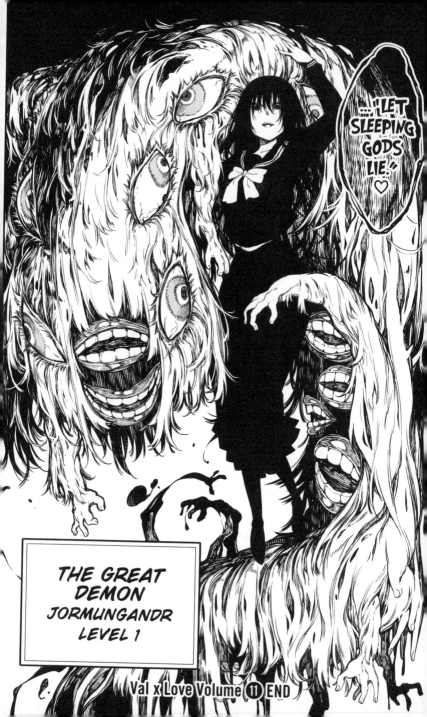

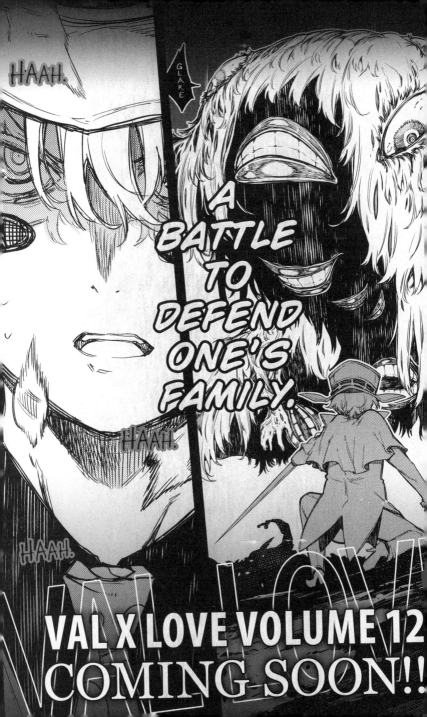

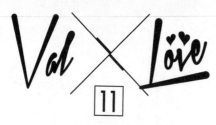

11

RYOSUKE ASAKURA

TRANSLATION: KO RANSOM
LETTERING: ROCHELLE GANCIO

VAL LOVE vol. 11
©2020 Ryosuke Asakura / SQUARE ENIX CO., LTD.
First published in Japan in 2020 by SQUARE ENIX CO., LTD. English translation rights arranged with SQUARE ENIX CO., LTD. and Yen Press, LLC through Tuttle-Mori Agency, Inc.

English translation © 2021 by SQUARE ENIX CO., LTD.

Yen Press
150 West 30th Street, 19th Floor
New York, NY 10001

Visit us at yenpress.com
facebook.com/yenpress
twitter.com/yenpress
yenpress.tumblr.com
instagram.com/yenpress

First Yen Press Edition: November 2021

Yen Press is an imprint of Yen Press, LLC.
The Yen Press name and logo are trademarks of Yen Press, LLC.

The publisher is not responsible for websites (or their content) that are not owned by the publisher.

Library of Congress Control Number: 2017954705

ISBNs: 978-1-9753-3643-1 (paperback)
        978-1-9753-3644-8 (ebook)

10 9 8 7 6 5 4 3 2 1

LSC-C

Printed in the United States of America